OOPS-A-NAVY

Navy SEAL Misadventure #1

a novel by

Gregg Bell

Prologue

New Navy SEALs Shelby Ryder and Earl Bernstein were from different worlds. Shelby, twenty-one, was from the grassy prairies of small town Kansas, and Earl, twenty-three, from the high art and culture world of big city Chicago. And truth be told, neither was too happy about being thrown together as partners. Shelby, a rare female SEAL, had a chip on her shoulder the size of Mt. Everest—her parents killed on vacation when their catamaran was sunk by a Russian submarine. She's a martial arts expert with a hair-trigger temper who survived the grueling Navy SEAL training exercise known as Hell Week by taking no guff from—and even knocking one guy out cold—her fellow male recruits. Earl, on the other hand, an artistic type obsessed with his health, spent most of his free time in the camp psychiatrist's office. During breaks in training, he'd self-diagnose his suspected diseases online and write poetry.

    The Navy brass paired them together in hopes of Earl being able to calm Shelby's violent tendencies and Shelby being able to help Earl with his mind. Things hadn't worked out that way. The brass even sent them on furlough to Hawaii in hopes of their finally bonding, but even that didn't produce the desired result. In desperation, they gave them one last chance. The mission seemed simple enough, but they never would have suspected how the stakes would escalate.

Chapter One

It was the best of times, it was the weirdest of times. And what a strange way for the new Navy SEAL partners' furlough in Hawaii to end. Shelby was visiting Earl in the hospital after she'd accidentally speared him when they'd gone spearfishing the night before. Of course, alcohol had been involved, but no matter, because now they had to get their act together in a hurry as they were due to leave Hawaii for Cuba on a top-secret op to rescue a US senator who'd disappeared there while playing golf.

Don Ho music played on the sound system in the hospital lobby that was decorated with paintings of Hawaiian kings and queens on horseback, and mannequins of hula dancers. But the hula dancers weren't shaking their hips like other hula dancers. Nothing titillating. This was a Catholic hospital. Our Lady of the Banzai Pipeline. Shelby walked to the information desk, where an elderly woman in a Hawaiian blouse and John Lennon glasses was vaping.

"Aloha," the woman said, exhaling vape through her nose.

"Yeah, okay." Shelby was in her Navy SEAL fatigues. She was under so much pressure. Here their first mission was coming up, and Earl gets in the way when she tried to spear a bonefish last night. But she resolved to be as nice as she could be to the little old lady doling out information. "I'm here to visit Earl Bernstein. He was injured in an accident last night at Laguna Haven Pier."

The woman set the vape behind her ear. "Let me see, okay, yes, I have an Earl Bernstein, but there's a police report here that says he was speared by an unknown assailant. Are you sure you have the right Earl Bernstein?"

Shelby knew she shouldn't be, but she was already beginning

to lose patience. "Yeah, it's gotta be the same one."

The information lady looked over her glasses. "Are you a relative?"

"His grandmother."

"No need to be smart, dear."

Shelby considered grabbing the registry and checking it herself, but she told herself to chill. "Just tell me his room number."

"He's on the E Komo Mai floor."

"Oh, come on, mom, do I look like I speak Japanese?" She tilted her head at the woman.

"You'd better show some respect, dear, or I'll call security."

Shelby counted to ten to calm down. She had no time for this. She and Earl had to be on a plane in two hours. "All right. Okay. Whatever you say."

"He's on the third floor. Room 317."

"The third floor. Room 317," Shelby mumbled as she walked toward the elevators. She was waiting for her hangover to ease and getting hungry. The elevator came.

She got off on the third floor and walked down the hall. It smelled of coconuts. She liked using coconut oil as a moisturizer, but the smell wasn't all that pleasant. "314," she said softly to herself. "315…316…ah 317." She walked in. Earl lay in bed, his left arm casted in an elevated sling dangling from a chain. He was sipping a tall drink with a little pink paper umbrella in it. A slice of chocolate cake was on the hospital tray next to his bed.

"Earl."

"Shelby."

She shrugged. "I hope you're not still mad about last night. Like I told you, it was an accident."

He took a deep breath. "I gotta be honest, Shelby. I *was* angry. But after I found out they were going to be able to save my arm I got over it."

"Well, that's good." The chocolate cake looked so appealing. She nodded toward it. "You gonna eat that?"

"Shelby." His tone spewed fatherly disappointment. "You're going to get called out for your weight when we get back to base."

"You sayin' I'm fat, Earl?"

"No, of course not, but all the time you spent lying around on the beach drinking Mai Tais has put on a few." Earl knew how volatile she could be and with only one functioning arm didn't want to set her off.

"Damn it, Earl, you gonna eat the cake or not?"

He sipped his drink. "Go ahead."

She took a bite. Mmm. It was that good kind of cake with frosting in the middle as well as on top. These Hawaiians really knew how to bake a cake. She polished it off, a smear of frosting on her lower lip. "I hope you're ready to get out of here. You know what's coming up."

"You got something on your lip." He pointed with his good arm.

"Earl."

"Okay, I was just saying."

"We have to be on a plane in two hours."

"Couldn't you have me excused?" He nodded toward his casted arm. "I mean, Cuba. I don't speak Spanish, there's no air conditioning and they have killer mosquitoes."

"Hey, need I remind you that you are a United States Navy SEAL?" She clenched her jaw.

He could feel her enthusiasm, her grit, strengthening him. "Yeah, that's right."

"Now get out of bed, lazy bones." She grabbed a towel, twirled it, and snapped it against his good arm. "We're booked on a C-130 Hercules for Florida. It leaves at 0-800."

"Okay, but on the other hand, the doctor said I really should take it easy for a few days."

"The doctor's not a SEAL, Earl." She detached his sling from the chain and examined the cast. "And you're not going to need this anymore. Your bones have probably set already."

"Really? Are you sure?"

"No, but you're a SEAL. And SEALs can handle anything."

Earl nodded. Her pep talk had him believing again. "Okay. Should we tell the doctors to remove it?"

"Nah, I've got a saw in the car."

* * *

When they arrived at the Navy SEAL base in Florida, the temperature was coolish for fall and it was raining. Sure, SEALs could handle that kind of weather, but still, Earl would've preferred to remain in the warmth and gentle trade winds of Hawaii to rest his damaged arm. And he felt he'd written several of his best poems there. He was planning on putting them in a little book and calling it "My Hawaiian Daydreams."

"Let's go, Earl." Shelby was testy after the long flight and took him by his good arm. "Admiral Gompers is ready to brief us."

They headed down a long corridor to the SEAL briefing room (actually the room was used for de-briefing as well), which was decidedly low-tech. Both SEALs knew Bull Gompers liked everything low-tech because Rear Admiral Bull Gompers was old school—and old. She had to be eighty-five if she was a day. In one corner of the room, a faded map of the Caribbean was pinned to a corkboard on an easel. Next to that stood a Navy SEAL mannequin in full combat gear, and in the other corner was a blackboard with a running total of the number of enemy kills SEALs had racked up in Cuba since World War II.

Shelby and Earl were amazed at how militarily strict, even

for a SEAL, Bull Gompers was. She wore a dress regalia Navy cap about the size of those little German hats you'd see regularly at Oktoberfests around the country in September. And then of course her dress blues. Her glasses were old-fashioned (but hey, they were probably new when she got them) with the frames blue on top and clear on the bottom. Her hair was gray going white and styled efficiently in a tight bun, and she was pacing the front of the room clutching a wooden ruler.

"Good to see you, SEALs." She stopped pacing and motioned with the ruler for Earl and Shelby to sit in the little school-like desks scattered about the room. "Hmm. Ryder, you're looking a little chunky."

"Yeah, well—"

"I'm sure you meant to say, *Yes, Admiral*."

"Yes, Admiral."

The rear admiral pursed her lips. "There are no fat SEALs, Ryder. Fat SEALs are walruses."

Earl cleared his throat. "Actually, I don't think that's accurate, Admiral—"

"I wasn't asking your opinion, Einstein."

"That's Bernstein, ma'am."

Bull frowned and continued, "Now let's get right to it. For starters, the area around Guantanamo…" And she pointed with the ruler to the US military base in Cuba on the map. "…hell, Cuba itself is full of Russian spies, poisoning the locals with their commie ideology. The damn commies want to take over the world, so you gotta keep your eyes peeled while you're there. But really, all this op requires of you is to find Senator Canfield and bring him back. Mission accomplished. Keep things just that simple."

"Should we liquidate any Russian spies we come across?" Shelby could hardly wait to see action.

Bull looked up at the ceiling and sighed. "Ryder, you're there to find the senator and bring him back, not cause an international incident."

Shelby nodded.

Again, Bull pointed to the map. "It's called *Yatera Seca*. Beats me what the hell that means, but that's what it's called. It's the golf course at Guantanamo, and the G.I.s there call it Lateral Hazard Golf Course, and it beats me why they call it that, as well. See, it's not really a golf course."

Earl raised a hand.

"What is it, Bernstein?"

"Why is it called a golf course, then?"

"I'm getting to that." Bull tapped the ruler three times into her palm. "Yes, thing is, it's hardly a golf course. Just some indoor-outdoor green mats set on the flat dusty earth. Just some lonely G.I.s' idea of making the place feel more like home. Damn Fidel Castro razed all the golf courses on the island because he saw them as symbols of capitalist excess. (Even though the commie himself loved to golf!) Currently, there is only one other golf course on the island, and it's a ritzy one and relatively close to Yatera Seca."

Earl shifted in his desk. "Admiral, with only the two courses, how is it no one has been able to find the senator?"

Bull adjusted her glasses. "That's what has everybody stumped, Einstein—"

"It's Bernstein, ma'am."

"Interrupt me again and you're off the mission!"

Earl didn't like that one bit. But for now, considering the thin ice Shelby and he were already on, he figured he'd better not press his luck. He folded his hands on the desk.

"So as I was *saying*," Bull continued, "the CIA, covert ops, dark ops, and even that basketball player Dennis Rodman—although Intel says he's come the closest—haven't been able to find the senator. All we know for a fact is that he was there on vacation, he played the Yatera Seca golf course, and then he was gone. Now are there any questions?"

Shelby grimaced. She knew this wouldn't be well received, but it was her biggest fear. "Admiral, are there any…are there any cannibals on the island?"

"Cannibals, Ryder? Are you serious?"

Shelby blushed and slunk down in her desk.

"Now let me make this perfectly clear." Bull gritted her teeth. "This is your last chance to stay SEALs. You screw up this mission, you're getting de-SEALed."

While Bull was talking, Earl's mind, as it was inclined to do, reverted to thinking about poetry, and he was wondering what might rhyme with Yatera Seca, well, what might rhyme with Seca actually. Seca…seca…seca. Let's see (his imagination was a-whirl). He tried the poem out in his mind.

Our first mission was at Yatera Seca / And things couldn't have looked any bleeka / A senator had gone there to golf and have fun / But that ain't what he's done.

"Einstein!" Bull smacked the chalkboard with the ruler. "Did you hear what I just said?"

He hadn't. "Yes, Admiral."

"And what was that?"

He shot Shelby a sidelong glance.

Shelby, doing her best ventriloquist, whispered, "She said if we screwed up we'd be de-SEALed."

"I believe you were saying if we failed the mission, ma'am, there was a chance we'd be de-SEALed."

"More than a chance, Einstein!" Bull tilted her cap ominously over one eye. "De-SEALed for sure!"

Chapter Two

"Why couldn't we have flown?" Shelby, looking over the twenty-six-foot bay boat, wasn't happy. "We gotta cross the Florida Straits in this piece of crap?"

"Well." Earl wore a captain's cap and, happy to be away from Bull Gompers, was relaxing a bit. "Because we don't want to belabor the obvious."

"Speak English, Earl."

"We have to sneak in. This boat will look like just another pathetic little Cuban fishing boat."

Shelby frowned but stepped into the boat. "If you say so."

Earl climbed the boat's little tower, from where he would steer. "Make sure you've got your life preserver on." The boat's seventy-horsepower engine kicked in, emitting a low gurgle.

"I smell exhaust." Shelby strapped the preserver over her bikini. "You sure the engine's working properly? I didn't survive Hell Week to die of asphyxiation."

"I think so." Earl put on blade sunglasses. "I rented it from somebody on Craigslist."

"Oh, that's reassuring."

"Just be sure to hang on when we leave the intracoastal waterway. The inlet where the ocean meets it can be a little choppy."

"Aye aye, Captain," Shelby said, rolling her eyes.

"All right now. Here we go."

The boat motored along smoothly through the intracoastal, multi-million-dollar homes on either side, yachts moored at private docks.

Shelby took photos of the palatial mansions with her phone. "They're not paying us enough, Earl. That's for damn sure."

Earl raised binoculars to his eyes. "Oh my."

"What?"

"Uh, nothing." He tried to sound calm. "It just looks like the ocean has a light chop."

"A light chop."

"Just to be on the safe side—better hang on to something."

Shelby ran to the front of the boat and looked out. "Oh… my…God!"

"The waves aren't *that big*."

The boat started rocking back and forth, dipping and rising as it headed into the rows of incoming waves.

"Not that big? We're going to die!"

"I told you to hang on to something."

"Hell, I'm not hanging on to anything because if I do, I won't be able to kill you!"

A wave crashed over the front of the boat and soaked Shelby. She grabbed the side railing to keep from being swept out to sea. "Earl!"

"I got this!"

But the boat rocked even more, smashing into the incoming swells and then plunging into their troughs. Only to smash even harder into the next swell.

"Yeah, sure you do!"

"Okay, we're almost out of it!"

The boat finally settled a bit.

"I never should've trusted you, Earl."

"Hey, this is where our SEAL training comes in, right?"

"It would if you knew what the hell you were doing."

They finally reached open water, and the ride evened out.

"Earl, look, porpoises!"

"Uh, Shelby, those are sharks."

"Great." Shelby sighed.

By nightfall, they were within range of the Cuban coast.

OOPS-A-NAVY

* * *

"Me llamo Shelby. My name is Shelby. *Como se llama?* What is your name?" Shelby read from her phone as they approached land. She pointed at Earl as he climbed down from the boat tower. *"Se llama goofball.* His name is goofball."

"Kill the light, Shelby, and put on your wetsuit. We're going to have to swim in from here."

"But what about the sharks?"

"Ah, as long as we're not bleeding, we'll probably be okay."

Shelby slipped into her wetsuit. *We'll probably be okay.* It felt good to feel the rubber against her body, like it hugged her. She watched Earl do the same. They strapped on masks, flippers and their Navy-issue waterproof backpacks, then plunged into the dark, warm water. Shelby thought she'd reached the shore first. She turned. "Earl?"

He was nowhere to be found. Nothing but the limitless blackness of the sea.

"Gotcha!" He jumped from behind a palm tree.

"Why, you nut. How did you get here before me?"

They hid their wetsuits, flippers and masks behind a palmetto bush, then jumped a couple of Cubans making out down the beach and stole their clothes.

"Should we kill them, Earl?"

"No, I don't think so." Earl gave his head a little shake. "They surrendered their clothes without a struggle." He nodded to the quivering couple nakedly clutching each other in the sand. *"Gracias, amigos."*

The Cubans nodded back but said nothing.

"We're off. Our first mission has officially begun!" Shelby led the way through the banyan trees. She didn't know exactly where the Yatera Seca golf course was but felt confident the GPS in her phone would get them there.

"I see lights up ahead beyond those coconut groves and swamps." Earl had out the binoculars. "I'm thinking the lights must be Yatera Seca."

"You're probably right. My phone says in two thousand yards you will have reached your destination."

"Cool." Earl wondered if there were crocodiles in the swamps. "Let's make our base camp here before we get too close to the swamps." He stopped walking. "In the morning, we'll see if there are golfers at Yatera Seca and hopefully we'll find Senator Canfield amongst them."

"Sounds good to me." Shelby pulled an inflatable tent from her backpack and activated the CO_2 power inflator cord. The tent filled with air and was not unlike those bounce playhouses rich people get for their bratty kids' birthday parties. "Wow," Shelby said as she stepped into the tent, her feet buoyant on the inflated floor, "these are really nice!"

"Yeah, how 'bout it?" Fondly remembering the birthday parties his parents had thrown him as a child, Earl began jumping up and down and bouncing off the walls. "Oh, Shelby, I'm reliving my youth! Won't you join me? C'mon!"

"Sure, why not." Shelby started bouncing. They joined hands and bounced until they heard what sounded like shots fired.

Earl quickly stopped their bouncing. "I hope they weren't shooting at the tent."

"I don't think they were." Shelby wiped the sweat from her brow and adjusted her peasant dress. "If they had been, the bullet holes would be deflating the tent by now."

"Right," Earl said, but nevertheless he widened his eyes. "Still, I think it would be wise to keep a low profile and bunk down for the night."

Shelby looked at him warily. "Which side of the tent you want?"

"Can't we huddle for warmth?"

OOPS-A-NAVY

"It's already warm." She scowled. "You too, Earl? The SEALs are already full of creepy gropers. I was hoping you'd be different."

He shook his head. "Nope. I fit right into the creepy-groper category."

"Well, you better control yourself with me or you'll be sorry."

Earl plopped down. "I'll take this side."

Shelby nodded. "And you'd better stay there."

* * *

The SEAL partners spent a good hour to hour and fifteen minutes in restless sleep before they started dreaming. Shelby dreamt she was doing the Macarena with Ethiopian guys who were using the dance as an opportunity to grope her. While Earl dreamt he was making out with Hillary Clinton. Desperate to exit her dream (Earl on the other hand wanted his to continue), Shelby woke, and when she did, she heard hissing outside the tent.

"Earl, wake up."

"What? Huh? What's up?"

"Listen."

"Shelby, I was having the best dream. I'm going back to sleep."

"No, listen. Don't you hear that?"

He groaned and pushed himself up on an elbow. "I don't hear anything."

Shelby rolled to his side of the tent. "You can't hear that hissing?"

"Shelby, your thigh is touching my…"

"Oh God!" She rolled back to her side.

"Now I'm returning to my dream."

"Whatever, Earl. There! You heard *that*, didn't you?"

"That's probably just some house cat that got loose, passing gas."

"Oh, I don't think so."

"If you don't feel safe, come back by me," he said, his voice full of lust.

"I don't think so, you perv."

"Then go to sleep and let me get back to my dream. Morning is going to come around before you know it."

"You're probably right." She rolled over and fell asleep. But the groping Ethiopians were waiting for her. What crap luck! She wondered what she'd done to deserve such a lousy dream. Then she felt it! Yes, she felt it! And she knew it wasn't part of her dream. No, Earl was rolling his tongue over her ankle, rolling his tongue all the way around it, and now his tongue was working its way up to her knee. Wow, he had a long tongue. She was going to kill him! She shook herself awake. "Earl, you degenerate!"

He bounded up and flicked on a lantern. "What's going on?!"

What the hell? He was on his side of the tent. Shelby looked down, and a huge slimy brown-spotted snake was wrapped around her ankle and swirling its way up her calf. And her leg was swelling as the snake squeezed with tremendous force.

Earl jumped up and unzipped the tent door.

"Earl, what are you doing?!"

"I'm getting out of here! That's a boa constrictor on your leg!"

"Aren't you going to help me?!"

"No." He stepped half out of the tent. "Good luck."

"Earl!!"

He frowned and made his way back in. "How'd you get it on your leg anyway?"

"I don't know! Just get it off!"

"You did nothing to attract it?"

"No!"

OOPS-A-NAVY

"How come I didn't get one on my leg?"

"Earl, my leg is turning blue!"

"That's what happens. They squeeze their prey to death."

"Well, help me!"

"If I do, you'll owe me."

"Okay, yes, anything!"

He took out his phone.

"What are you doing? Who you calling?"

"Just shut up for a minute. You're hysterical."

Shelby resolved that if she lived, she'd kill Earl in the most gruesome way imaginable.

Earl searched the Internet for "how to remove a boa constrictor from a sleeping person's leg." And yeah, well, Shelby wasn't sleeping anymore, but she'd just woken him and it was the best he could come up with. He found something called "how to survive an attack by a boa constrictor if you're sleepy." He was amazed by the stuff you could find online.

"Earl!"

"Okay already." The article said to put the person's leg into a bucket of water, and the snake would be afraid of drowning and release its grip. "Do you have a bucket?"

"What?"

"Okay, I'm assuming you don't. I don't either." He grabbed her under the arms.

"Hey, you creep!"

"Shelby, I'm not groping this time."

By now the snake had wrapped itself to above her knee. "Okay, but if you are, you won't live to see the morning."

He picked her up. "Oh geez, you really have put on weight."

"That's not fair, Earl. I'm in a really vulnerable situation here."

"Well, still, you weigh a ton." He carried her out to the swamp.

"*What are* you doing?"

"Sticking your leg in the swamp."

"What the hell for?!"

"Just trust me." He stuck her leg in the swamp.

Shelby grimaced. The water was cold and icky and probably filled with parasites entering her pores and making her infertile. Not that she was dead-set on having kids, but it would be nice to have the option. "It's not letting go."

"Give it time."

"Give it time?!"

"It can only hold its breath for so long."

"How long?"

Earl took out his phone again. "How long can a boa constrictor hold its breath underwater?" he asked it. He found one of those sites that make you click several times to get the full answer. *Click.* "It says there are many variables."

"Earl!"

"Okay, okay." *Click.* "It says baby boa constrictors can't hold their breaths as long as adults."

"Earl!!"

Click. "Oh, you're not gonna like this one."

"What does it say?"

"It says…twenty minutes."

"Earl, what's that?"

A murky presence silently streamed toward Shelby in the swampy darkness. Earl turned his phone's spotlight onto it.

Shelby shivered. "What is it?"

"A crocodile."

Shelby pulled her leg from the swamp.

"No!" He put her leg back. "The twenty minutes will be up soon." He waded into the swamp and faced down the prehistoric beast, but the croc wasn't used to being stood up to in the pre-dawn hours, so it slunk away, perhaps berating itself for backing down. Earl didn't care if it felt bad.

"Earl, I think it's finally letting go."

"See." He raised her leg. Indeed, the snake's lungs were puffing in and out, gasping for air, and Earl was able to remove it. Then, adhering to the Navy SEAL Code of Reptile Catch and Release (RCR), he released the winded snake safely into the wild.

Earl carried Shelby, her leg a blue swollen mess that was grossing him out, back to the tent. They entered, and he zipped the door behind them and laid Shelby down, well, actually he dropped her a little and she bounced. He hadn't meant to drop her, but she *had* put on weight. "I think it's ironic that I almost lost my arm in the spearfishing accident," he said, settling on his side of the tent, "and now you're going to lose your leg."

"Do you really think I'm going to lose it?"

"Yeah, for sure."

"Oh God."

"Just be grateful. If I hadn't helped you, you'd be dead."

Shelby considered what it would be like to face life with only one leg. Then she thought Earl was right—at least she was alive. And ultimately, he *had* helped her, and he'd been especially decent facing down the croc in the swamp. "Okay, yeah."

Earl belched.

Shelby rolled onto her side to face him. "But, Earl?"

"What?"

"It was decent of you to save me from the croc."

He belched again and drifted off to sleep, continuing his dream of making out with Hillary Clinton.

Chapter Three

The next morning was sweltering but despite the heat, Earl and Shelby counted themselves lucky to have all their limbs. They walked out into the bright sunshine, and Earl grabbed a machete, climbed a palm tree and cut down some coconuts so they'd have something fresh to eat.

"How's your leg?" He hacked open a coconut.

"Oh." She sat on a tree stump and pulled her hair into a ponytail. "I think it's coming back to life. I can feel the circulation returning."

"I'm surprised. I was thinking I'd need to amputate it." He hacked open another coconut. "So, time to find the golfing senator everybody is making such a fuss over, huh?" He laughed, put a straw in one of the coconuts and handed it to Shelby. "Who knew our first mission would be so important?" He rolled his eyes.

"Yeah, such a lightweight mission, but we gotta make it work, Earl, because if I get de-SEALed, I won't be able to avenge my parents, and man, that's absolutely everything to me."

Earl pried the husk off a coconut. "You know, I really think you get too emotional about this."

"About what?"

"This bit about your parents being killed by the Russian sub."

"This *bit*?"

"Well, stuff happens, Shelby. All is fair in love and war."

"Earl, they were catamaraning on vacation!"

He shrugged. "Still, you're a SEAL. You should be able to put that behind you, especially since it's clouding your judgment."

Shelby smirked. "Thank you, Doctor Freud."

OOPS-A-NAVY

"Hey, I'm just saying you need to take it easy."

"Yeah, take it easy. Easier said than done." She blew out an exhalation and took a sip of the cool coconut milk.

"So, do you know how to play golf?" He tossed the coconut husk into some bushes.

"Sort of. My parents took me a couple of times to a putt-putt place that had a driving range."

"I'll take that as a no."

"I can hit the ball—sometimes."

Earl dug coconut out with a utility knife. "I guess I really shouldn't talk, because I'm pretty much the same. My parents tried to get me to take lessons from the pro at our country club, and I took a few, but my heart wasn't in it. All I wanted to do was write poetry."

"So if that's all you wanted to do, why didn't you become a poet?"

"Well." He noshed on a chunk of coconut. "I needed stuff to write about. I needed adventure."

Shelby's phone beeped. "Hey, I just got a text saying the G.I.s at Guantanamo are holding a couple sets of golf clubs for us."

"That was thoughtful of them."

"Wow, I wasn't expecting that. Nice to have some inter-services goodwill."

"Yeah, surprising, considering how the other branches of the military are so jealous of SEALs."

"Uh-huh." Shelby stood. "You ready to go?"

"I gotta floss my teeth first. I think some coconut shards got in there, and I'm afraid I'll have pocketing in my gums."

Shelby blew the bangs off her forehead. "All right but hurry."

Earl flossed and brushed his teeth (and used anti-cavity rinse), then they set out for the Yatera Seca golf course.

To be on the safe side, they'd chosen to dress in fatigues

rather than bathing suits. It was a jungle after all and best to be prepared. But as they ventured deeper in, before long, they wished they'd brought their machetes as it was tough getting through the gnarly jungle underbrush without them.

A thicket rustled. They whirled to look. When they turned back, ten or twelve savages were pointing spears at them. And they had very unfriendly looks on their faces. The savages were bare-chested, war paint covering their bodies, and wore various kinds of knee-length surfer swim trunks. (But Shelby and Earl were quite sure they weren't surfers.) They also wore headdresses of various types. Mostly headbands, colorful though, and a few wore baseball caps turned backward. A tall guy had some kind of straw thing on his head. Like a clump of grass had been growing there and died and dried out.

"Hey, who are you guys?" Shelby understandably asked.

Earl thought that was a reasonable question too.

But the savages weren't answering. They just brandished their spears.

"Do you speak English?" Earl inquired.

"Let's kill them," said the guy with the dead bush on his head. "They are condescending Americans certainly."

Earl and Shelby squinted at each other, wondering who the savages might be.

Finally Shelby said, "I don't know. I think they might be soccer hooligans. All that body paint and threatening violence. If they start singing patriotic songs we'll know for sure."

Earl shook his head. "I think it's more likely they're from a rainforest tribe."

"Oh, that's so farfetched, Earl."

"No more farfetched than soccer hooligans."

"Yes it is."

"No it isn't."

Seemingly resenting being left out of the conversation, one of the savages said, "In order to pass, you must give payment."

"Yeah, sure, buddy." Earl laughed and looked the guy in the eye. "Do you take MasterCard?"

Shelby flushed red. "What are you talking about, Earl? We don't have MasterCard. Only American Express."

"Shelby, I was kidding him."

"Quiet!" yelled a savage who had apparently tired of brandishing his spear and was now leaning his chin on the weapon's butt end, using it as a post.

Shelby felt it was time to make a move. "Earl," she whispered, "do you have Scrabble in your backpack?"

"Sure." He nodded. "But I was figuring we'd save that for a rainy day. I don't think we should play now."

"Well, I don't wanna play now, but lemme have it, will ya?"

He unzipped his backpack.

"What are you doing?!" said the tree-hat savage. "No move!"

"That should be 'don't move,'" Earl corrected, wagging his forefinger at the man. "Bad grammar can really inhibit your chances of rising in life."

A spear flew at Earl's head and he ducked just in time. He remembered Shelby spearing him in Hawaii and said, "If I get speared again, I am not going to be happy."

"Just relax, Earl." Shelby knew it took a lot for him to get angry, but once he did, he could be one uber-violent SEAL. "Nobody's getting speared. Just hand me the Scrabble."

Earl gave her the board game.

"Okay, guys." Shelby smiled big. "I have a proposition for you. Let us, as a gesture of friendship and goodwill, barter our Scrabble game for safe passage." She thought for a moment. "It's either that or we'll have to kill you."

Earl asked, "You'd really kill them?"

"Well, I'm giving them a way out. Now the ball is in their court." She walked toward them with the game.

The savages brandished their spears ferociously.

"No, no," Shelby called. "It's just a board game, savages. It won't hurt you." She opened the box and showed them the colorful playing board and all the little wooden squares with letters on them.

"I'd take her up on it," Earl encouraged. "If you get her angry, you'll be sorry."

The savages slowly stopped brandishing their spears and gathered around the game. One of them with his cap on backward said, "This looks like it could be fun!"

"It's really fun!" Earl chimed in.

The savages picked up the little wooden squares, scratching their long, dirty fingernails across them, biting down on them with brown teeth. They huddled. Their heads started nodding. When the huddle broke, the tree-hat savage said, "Deal. We get Scrabble. You pass."

Earl suddenly experienced buyer's remorse. "But, Shelby, what will we do on rainy days?"

"Well, we have to let them have it now, Earl, otherwise we could—like Bull warned us—have an international incident on our hands." Shelby was adamant. "The Huff Post or CNN will probably hear about it, and then, you know, the ACLU loves defending savages, and we'd be up a creek without a paddle."

"Well, yeah, when you put it that way."

"Okay, savages, here we come." Shelby, trailed by Earl, breached their midst, the savages grumbling but parting.

* * *

Shelby and Earl walked on. As they passed a swamp, Earl was still brooding on giving the Scrabble game to the savages. And it was taking them forever to trudge through the jungle without their machetes.

OOPS-A-NAVY

The swamp reminded Shelby of Earl saving her from the croc, and she got to thinking that after some serious cowardice, Earl really had risked his life for her. "Thank you, Earl. Really. Thank you."

Despite their glaring differences, there were nevertheless times Earl felt as if he and Shelby had a true psychic connection. This wasn't one of those times. "Whatever."

The blistering heat pulverized them as they trudged on (although neither of them had blisters), their fatigue T-shirts soaked with sweat, looking nearly black. Fortunately, they'd been through so much brutality (ninety-five percent of the recruits who started Navy SEAL Hell Week dropped out before it was over and of those that remained eighty-five percent died) it wasn't much of a problem for them—but they would've preferred it to have been cooler.

Just as they saw a break in the jungle canopy and sensed they were near the golf course, Earl felt a mosquito bite his shoulder. At least he thought it was a mosquito. In reality, he'd been struck with a poison-drug dart from a blowgun hunter. "Shelby, I've been bitten by a really aggressive mosquito. I hope I don't get the Zika virus."

"Well, come on, Earl, I'll spray some lemon eucalyptus on you to keep the mosquitoes off." She pulled a spray pump bottle from her backpack and spritzed him.

"Ah! Don't get it in my eyes!"

"Don't worry, it's all natural. The Navy would never give us anything dangerous."

"I don't care. I don't want it in my eyes."

"Okay, okay." She quit spraying it directly into his face but thoroughly doused the rest of him with the repellent. She knew the Zika virus was dangerous and that the commie mosquitoes would be only too happy to infect a Navy SEAL.

But Earl now smelled like a lemon orchard. "God, Earl, you

really stink."

"Well, yeah," he said, trying to wipe the pungent liquid off. "What do you expect after you practically hosed me down with the stuff?"

"I didn't use that much. It was only a twenty-ounce bottle and I used a little over half." She held her nose. "I'm going to walk up ahead. You trail me by fifty yards."

Oh great, Earl thought, and here was the golf course coming up. "Fine." But he was feeling woozy and nauseous from the poison-drug blow dart. "I think the lemon eucalyptus smell is making me sick."

"Yeah, it's making me sick too." Shelby hurried ahead. But when she turned back, Earl was staggering. She waited for him to catch up and removed some Navy-regulation charcoal from her backpack. "Here, this will help." She rubbed the charcoal on his face. "You look like a black guy now, but at least the lemon smell should be off your face."

"Thanks, Hillary."

"You just called me Hillary."

"No, I didn't."

"Yes, you did."

Earl knew something was wrong with his mind. He probably did call her Hillary because of his dream last night. In fact, he felt as if he was in a dreamlike state now. Like the world wasn't solid anymore. It was porous, Harry Potter-like. "I'll watch it from now on."

"You do that. And get ready to play golf."

* * *

A couple of Army grunts, at least they looked like grunts, were on one of the holes of the Yatera Seca golf course.

"Come on, Earl." Shelby was excited. "Let's go say hi."

OOPS-A-NAVY

"I don't know, Hillary."

"I'm not Hillary." She cuffed him. "Oh look, I got charcoal on my hand."

Nothing was working for Earl lately. And not only was he calling Shelby Hillary, but she was also starting to look like Hillary too. (Although, in his dream, he was attracted to the former Secretary of State.) Still, he recognized he wasn't himself. His mind was moving so slow.

"Get a grip, will you, Earl?" Shelby frowned. "We have to talk to these grunts, and I don't want to come off as losers."

The world was tingling all around Earl. Stars shimmered in his peripheral vision and everything kept slowing down. "Yep, yep, I'm on it." But he wasn't.

Shelby called to the grunts. "Yo, golfers. Mind if we join up?"

The grunts were bare chested, and when they saw Shelby, they started subtly flexing their biceps.

Oh great, Shelby thought. Here I am in the middle of nowhere and more horny guys. She took Earl by the elbow of his bad arm and dragged him along. "Now remember, we're on a top-secret mission. Don't reveal anything to these grunts."

"Right, Hill."

She squeezed his arm, hard. "Call me that again and I'll break it."

The huskier of the two grunts said, "Yeah, come on over. We'd love to have a foursome."

"Guys." Shelby blushed. "Thanks for the offer but I have to tell you, we're not into kinky sex. I don't know what you Army boys do down here in Cuba—that's your business—but we in the Navy live by a strict code of honor."

"We weren't talking about sex," said the less-husky grunt, who looked a little like Earl, with the charcoal streaks he had under his eyes, or maybe he looked like a short, sweaty Tom

Brady. "We just meant four players in a group, which is what you want in golf."

"Oh, that's right." Shelby smiled. It sounded right anyway.

The huskier grunt was sizing Shelby up like a piece of horseflesh. "But if you wanted to do the other foursome…"

"Ha, ha, grunt." Shelby laughed but she wasn't happy. The grunt could take it as far as he wanted—at his peril.

The less-husky grunt spoke up. "Who's the catatonic-looking guy?"

Shelby had practically forgotten about Earl. She turned to him. He just stood there soaked with sweat like someone with no bus fare waiting for a bus in a thunderstorm, except there was no thunderstorm or bus. "Earl." She let go of his arm, hoping he'd move around a little and act normal.

"What?"

Shelby turned to the grunts. "I'm Shelby Ryder. And this is Earl Bernstein."

The grunts introduced themselves.

Earl managed to shake hands, but he didn't know if he'd be able to do much else, his mind barely functioning. Still, he was a SEAL and determined to try. "It's sure hot here in Afghanistan."

Shelby looked at him. What the hell! She turned to the grunts. "Come on, guys, let's play some golf!"

The grunts gave each other a strange look, but they led the SEALs to the next hole. Being a woman, they let Shelby tee off first. She didn't take it as condescension. Even though she was a SEAL, she was a lady first and liked to be treated with respect. She took a big swing with the golf club the huskier grunt had lent her and missed the ball. But she connected with the next swing.

Next up, the grunts hit their shots.

Now—oh God—it was Earl's turn. Shelby felt like time stood still as Earl hunched over the ball staring at it. It was as if he'd been entranced by a snake charmer. He just kept staring and staring, and after a while the grunts started laughing. Finally, he turned the club sideways and started strumming it as if it were a ukulele.

Shelby jumped in. "Oh, Earl, you're such a joker." She snatched the club from him and tossed it to the grunts. "Earl was the top-rated comedian at our base's talent show." She grabbed him by his bad arm and yanked him along. "Come on, funny man, that's enough joking for now."

They made it through three holes before Earl collapsed onto the dusty earth. He was panting. His skin, wherever the charcoal wasn't covering it, was fiery red. Shelby touched his forehead. It was blazing. She figured then that something might be wrong with him. She turned to the grunts. "I'm thinking Earl may have succumbed to malaria. Would you help me get him to the medic's?"

Chapter Four

The base doctor had long silvery hair folding over the collar of his white lab coat, a black shirt under that. He sported a very gray goatee, had a pot gut and a serious limp, the stethoscope draped around his neck swaying as he walked. He peeled back one of Earl's eyelids and shined a flashlight.

"That's really bright." Earl blinked.

Shelby looked at the doctor's name tag. "Can you tell what's wrong with him, Doctor Cooke?" Her phone beeped and she checked it.

"Please, call me Oscar." The doctor shined the flashlight into Earl's other eye. "And I'm not sure about the rest of him, but he can see."

"Well, that's good." Shelby yawned—the call had been another telephone solicitor wanting to know if she'd donate her car to charity—and slipped the phone into her pocket.

The doctor removed Earl's sweaty T-shirt.

Almost as an afterthought, Earl said, "A mosquito bit me on my shoulder. Could that have anything to do with this?"

"I'll check," said the doctor, circling around. "Oh no!"

Shelby leaned on a medicine cabinet. "Is it a tumor, doc?"

The physician pulled his hair into a ponytail. "Worse."

"The Zika virus?" Shelby knew she should've sprayed him with the lemon eucalyptus earlier.

"Worse."

Earl fainted.

"What the hell." Shelby shrugged. "Why did he do that?"

"It's okay. This'll wake him up." Doctor Cooke threw a glass of ice water into Earl's face.

"But what's wrong with him, doctor?" Shelby would need to

report to Bull.

"Please, call me Oscar," the doctor intoned.

"Oscar."

"Well, look here." The physician took a black magic marker from his pocket and circled the little wound on Earl's shoulder.

"Is that permanent ink?" Shelby asked. It looked like permanent ink.

"Yes," said the doctor, "but no one will see it here, and he probably won't live anyway."

"Probably won't *live*?" Earl was wide-awake now.

"Calm down, soldier," Doctor Cooke advised. "I just said *probably*. There's still a slight chance you'll survive."

"Oh great." Earl smirked. He was thinking, yeah, his parents were right—he should've been a proctologist.

"Anyway." The doctor nodded Shelby over. "See where I've circled?"

Shelby leaned in. "Yes."

The doctor, with a practiced move, pulled a magnifying glass from his lab coat and hovered it over the area. "Well, look closer."

"Okay."

"See?"

"See what?"

"It's more than a mosquito bite." The doctor drew three arrows to the specific spot. "Now?"

"Yeah, now I see, but if you keep drawing those lines he's going to look like a gangbanger."

"Eh." The doctor slipped the magic marker into his pocket. "People will just think it's some kind of satanic tattoo."

"Okay, but is that a good thing?"

The doctor shrugged. "Anyway, yeah, that's not a mosquito bite. It's the wound from a poisoned and drugged blow dart."

"Blow dart?!" Shelby shuddered.

"Blow dart?" Earl echoed but was unable in his poisoned,

drugged state to match the same level of Shelby's wonderment. In fact, he was fading fast.

"Blow dart," Dr. Cooke confirmed.

An ominous silence filled the office.

Finally Shelby said, "So what's in a blow dart?"

The physician swallowed. "Probably fentanyl, angel dust, strychnine and Coca Cola."

"Coca Cola?"

"It's the Real Thing."

"I know what it is but why Coca Cola?"

"The carbonation makes the poison spread faster."

"Wait, wait, this is crazy." Shelby confronted the doctor. "Blow dart? How the hell did he get hit by a blow dart?"

"The rainforest people." The doctor didn't flinch.

"There are rainforests here?" Shelby's eyes filled with amazement as she realized Earl had been right about there being rainforest people.

The doctor remained calm. "Well, I don't know if they meet the Wikipedia definition, but Cuba has forests and it rains in them, so in that sense it has de facto rainforests."

"All right," Shelby said, but she didn't let on that she didn't know what "de facto" meant—she didn't want the doctor thinking she was from Kansas.

The physician fingered his stethoscope. "You didn't encounter any primitive people?"

"Not that I recall," Shelby said. "Wait, now that you mention it, we did encounter a few. In fact, we had to give up our Scrabble game to get by them."

"Aaah." The doctor nodded knowingly. "They do that all the time. Then when they can't figure out how to play the games, they put them on eBay."

"I'll have to check if it's there." Shelby grabbed her phone. "But hang on, maybe we should take care of Earl first? He seems to have slipped into a coma."

"That's probably a good idea. Besides, the game might not be on eBay yet."

Shelby put the phone back into her pocket. Yeah, eBay could wait. She wasn't going to buy the Scrabble back anyway. If she did, where would they ship it? "Just what are you suggesting we do, doctor?"

"About the game or Earl?"

"Earl."

"Well." The doctor, a pained look on his face, rubbed his goatee and dandruff drifted down—it was easy to see against his black shirt. "I'm afraid there's only one thing *to* do. We, well, I, have to dig deeply into his back to take a biopsy to determine what the poison drug is, so I can give him an antidote."

"Okay."

"But it's going to be excruciatingly painful."

"That's all right."

"I'm not going to be able to give him anesthetic."

"Why not?"

"Because it might interact with the fentanyl and kill him instantly."

Shelby frowned. "I thought you weren't sure there was fentanyl in his system."

"I'm not, but what if there is? Would you want to take the chance?"

Shelby nodded. "Sure."

"Well, so would I, but I'm afraid it's not up to us. Only Earl can decide." The doctor shook Earl out of his stupor and explained the dire situation.

Earl wasn't happy about it, but he agreed to have the procedure done. Or at least it seemed as if he did. Kind of a semi-coma nod anyway.

The doctor asked Shelby to move, opened a drawer in the

medicine cabinet, took out a pamphlet and handed it to her. "Now you can help by reading him this *Guided Imagery for Those Undergoing Agonizingly Painful Surgery Without Anesthetic* pamphlet."

Earl seemed to revive a bit. He was sweating. "Agonizingly painful?"

"Well, yes," the doctor said, stroking his goatee. "But you *could* pass out from the pain, and after that you won't feel a thing."

Earl rolled his eyes. "Great."

"Okay, I'm ready with the reading." Shelby was excited. She once took an anger management class where they did this kind of thing.

"Are we good to go, then?" The doctor grabbed a scalpel and wiped it on his lab coat.

"Wait a minute." Earl held up a palm. "I can't do this."

"Earl, you're a SEAL," Shelby said. "At least give this guided imagery stuff a try. It looks really good."

Earl frowned but nodded weakly.

Shelby told Earl to repeat after her and started reading. "I joyfully accept this pain experience…"

He cleared his throat. "I joyfully accept this pain experience…"

The doctor moved in with the scalpel. "Now hold still."

"Aahhhhhhhh!"

"Earl, I didn't do anything yet."

"But I felt something."

"That was just my finger."

"Oh, okay. I guess I'm a little sensitive." Sweat dripped from his forehead onto the exam table.

"All right, Earl, I'm going to read again. Just repeat after me." Shelby held up the pamphlet. "There is nothing I need to do but be present in this moment…"

OOPS-A-NAVY

"There is nothing I need to do but—Aahhhhhhhh!"

Shelby continued, "I imagine cool, refreshing ice packs on my area of pain…"

"I imagine cool—Aahhhhhhhh!"

"There, that should do it." The doctor extracted a chunk of flesh with the scalpel, blood dripping, but not a lot, onto the floor.

"Oh my God." Earl was panting. "That hurt *so* much."

The doctor caught Earl's eye. "Now I just need to take another one a little deeper."

Earl slumped on the exam table.

"Just kidding, Earl. Ha ha. We're done. You can put your T-shirt back on." The doctor sat on a little stool and slid over to a microscope, put Earl's flesh on a slide and whisked it in. "Now we'll see what the heck is inside you and give you an antidote, then you'll be on your way."

"That's awesome, doc." Shelby had had enough with Earl being such a helpless blow dart victim.

"Oh no!" The doctor was intensely focused, looking into the microscope.

"What?" Earl was trembling.

The doctor pushed back on the stool. "Well, I've got good news and bad news."

Earl breathed in slowly. "Okay, the good news?"

"There is no fentanyl."

"Phew!" Earl laughed. "But…the bad?"

"I've never seen a strain like this before." The doctor clasped his hand on Earl's shoulder.

"Ahhhh!"

"Sorry, I forgot that was your bad one." He put his hand on Earl's other shoulder. "What's in you is a secret poison drug from the primitive people on the island."

"Really?"

"There is no known antidote and chances are overwhelming

you'll die."

Earl fainted.

"So what does this mean, Oscar?" Shelby was proud of remembering to use the physician's first name. "If he manages to live for a while, how should I be expecting him to act?"

"Well, a wide range of symptoms are possible." The doctor sat at his desk. "Paranoia, sore throat, tingling in the extremities, a persecution complex, multiple personality disorder, sudden death, and ingrown toenail."

"That doesn't sound so bad."

"No, not at all."

"Can you help me get him up from the floor?"

Chapter Five

It was the next morning. The night before, Shelby had managed to get Earl back to the tent from the doctor's office, but now she was wondering what Earl's mental instability from the blow dart poison drug would do to their mission. He seemed like a time bomb. Like he could explode at any moment and botch things, and if they didn't get Senator Canfield back, they were getting de-SEALed.

Yeah, how would it all play out? Outside the tent, she was cooking oatmeal over a little fire made of dried palm fronds. The sun filtered through the jungle canopy, streaming shadowy light. Would Earl stay sane? Would he even stay alive? Would he get an ingrown toenail? She gave him a bowl of oatmeal. "Here you go." (He took it okay.) But the most pressing question now was, would he be able to play golf because not having found Senator Canfield at Yatera Seca, they had to go to the nicer course, and the nicer course would require a higher level of playing ability.

"How's the oatmeal?"

He breathed in quickly and nodded. "It could use brown sugar but the texture is excellent."

"I'll see if I can get some brown sugar." But his reply was encouraging. Lucid. Maybe things wouldn't be that bad after all. "So I was thinking we'd head to the better golf course, and I'm sure Senator Canfield will be there as it's the only other course on the island."

"Oh." Earl stuck his spoon into the oatmeal and set the bowl down. "I was hoping to have a day or two to myself. You know, after yesterday's trauma. Maybe write some poetry. Think you could go by yourself?"

"Yeah, sure." Okay, she'd had it with coddling his lazy bones already. Hey, she'd *tried* to be tolerant. It hadn't worked. "I'll just call Bull Gompers and tell her you want to sit here and write poems all day."

"Well no, don't do *that*."

"Hey, you're a SEAL, Earl! So big deal—some rainforest savage shot you with a poison-drug blow dart and you'll probably die. Shake it off!"

He took another bite of the oatmeal and a deep breath. "You're right, Shelby. Thanks. You always straighten me out. Yeah, let's go play some golf! I mean, look for Senator Canfield!"

Earl dressed in yellow- and blue-striped shorts (that might have been swim trunks—Shelby wasn't sure), a candy-apple red Polo shirt and an Australian outback hunting hat, while Shelby wore a cute little white tennis dress. They grabbed their machetes and headed into the jungle. Shelby knew from Bull Gomper's map that the other golf course, although nearby, was on the ocean, which Shelby, being from Kansas, immensely looked forward to seeing. Yes, taking in the ocean would be a nice side benefit to playing golf, er, looking for Senator Canfield.

After an hour of hacking their way through palmetto bushes and banana trees, they emerged from under the jungle canopy. Now they could see the sign for De La Rata Country Club. They hid their machetes in some bushes and kept walking.

Wow, Shelby thought, the clouds floated over the ocean in a line paralleling the shore. Soon enough she heard the breakers rolling in. Palm trees surrounded the multimillion-dollar clubhouse, and at the edge of the property stood a tremendous fountain, with several levels, pouring tons of water down in endless, cascading sheets that ended in a pool at each level. Atop the fountain sat the De La Rata Grill, a ritzy outdoor restaurant swarming with waiters in tuxedos, catering to overweight vacationing Americans. Let's face it, though, Shelby thought, although gaudy, elitist and mindlessly materialistic, the country

OOPS-A-NAVY

club *was* much nicer than Yatera Seca. And it was amazing that such a beautiful establishment could be so near a wild jungle. She was glad she'd called ahead to reserve a tee time. Now if only Earl wouldn't go nutso or die on her.

Couples drove by in golf carts. The women with svelte figures and sleeveless tops showing off their buff arms, the men sporting gold watches and finely weathered tans. Shelby was tempted to zone out and keep enjoying the vibe of the place, but ever the professional soldier, she determined to find out what she could, at least a little bit, about Senator Canfield's whereabouts first.

They checked in at the pro shop and were scheduled to play with another couple. Shelby reminded Earl to maintain their cover (they were dentist colleagues from Cleveland), let her do most of the talking and keep his head on straight.

"I'm good. I'm good," he said. "I'm feeling hardly delusional at all."

She wondered about that statement—was he putting her on? —but there was no time. The other couple approached. They looked like they belonged. Like you could take a photo of them and put it on a postcard for the country club. The man, in a royal blue Polo, khaki shorts, brown anklet socks and expensive alligator golf shoes, smiled confidently. The woman, a shapely blonde, wore a mauve top and pastel pink calypso pants. They introduced themselves. They were the Harringtons, Preston and Ashley. They were Americans, but they also owned a vacation home on the island and were members of De La Rata.

Preston sidled over to make small talk while Ashley hit her tee shot. "So, what do you two do?"

As if hurrying to answer they both said, "We're dentists."

"Ha ha, interesting," Preston said. Ashley hit her shot, and he called to her, "Ashley, what do you know, they're dentists!" He turned back to Shelby and Earl. "Ashley is a dentist too."

"Nice," Earl said, thinking she really was kind of hot.

Shelby gave her fellow SEAL a *keep it together, Earl* look.

"Wonderful! Small world." Ashley smiled broadly, walking over. "What sort of dentistry do you practice?"

Preston headed to the tee and took some practice swings.

Earl smiled. "We work on people's teeth."

Ashley laughed. "Well, I would hope so. Of course, there are a few veterinarian dentists."

Shelby, thinking about the potential effects of the poison-drug blow dart on her fellow SEAL, said, "Earl does stand-up comedy on the side. You'll have to excuse him as he's always *on*."

"I see," Ashley said, but she was waiting for an answer from Shelby.

"Uh, of course. I have a children's practice, and Earl teaches dentistry at Midtown Community College."

"He teaches dentistry *at a community college*? But you need a bachelor's degree to even go to dental school."

"I know, I know." Shelby gritted her teeth. "But Midtown is an experimental program in the inner city where they waive the need for academic credentials to encourage more gangbangers to become dentists. Earl actually founded it just recently."

"Huh."

"Oh, look." Shelby saw Preston had hit his shot. "I guess I'm up next." She hurried to the tee.

In the meantime, Earl said to Ashley, "Actually, we're Navy SEALs on a top-secret mission."

Ashley laughed. "Oh, you *are* funny."

Shelby returned and stealthily whacked Earl with her driver on his bad arm. "You're up."

"He's a stitch," Ashley confided to Shelby as Earl walked off holding his arm.

Shelby nodded. "What did he say to you when I was teeing

OOPS-A-NAVY

off?"

"Oh." She chuckled. "He said you were Navy SEALs on a top-secret mission."

Shelby burned, fearing their cover was blown.

"So, Shelby," the elegant woman said, "in your children's practice, what age range do you treat?"

Shelby frowned. "Oh, any."

"Wow. That's impressive."

Shelby was going to brain Earl. He was standing on the tee taking practice swing after practice swing, then stopping to toss blades of grass into the air to test the wind direction as if he were Tiger Woods. *Come on already!* This dentist talk was making her so uncomfortable.

"So." Ashley again. "Where do you stand on thumb sucking?"

"Oh." What the hell! "Uh, I haven't done it since I was little."

Ashley laughed. "Well, I can see Earl isn't the only comedian. But seriously, don't you think when the permanent teeth come in, thumb sucking can lead to misalignment?"

"Oh, yes, I do think that. Yes."

Earl finally hit his shot, and they mercifully took off in their golf carts. Earl seemed to be reviving a bit and even enjoying himself because of Ashley, but Shelby was on tenterhooks, dreading whatever crazy thing he might say next.

On the back nine, Ashley got Shelby off to the side and said, "It's been fun getting to know you a little, and, well, we tell everyone we meet that if you happen to know anything about Senator Canfield's whereabouts—he used to be a regular member of our foursome whenever he visited—please tell us, because we miss him terribly."

Say what? Shelby nearly fainted. She didn't know how to answer but she had to say something. "I heard he was gone but what happened to him?"

Ashley shrugged. "Nobody knows. But I'll tell you one thing, I for damn sure am determined to find out."

Shelby watched Earl. He had his arm around Preston and was telling him something. "Actually, Ashley, uh, being Americans, we're very interested in finding Senator Canfield too."

"Really?"

Shelby nodded. Oh God, what was Earl telling Preston?

"And why is that, Shelby?"

"Well, uh, because we really like the senator's stance on whether gay bakery owners should have to sell wedding cakes to born-again Christians."

"Ah, I hear you. That's in front of the Supreme Court now, isn't it?"

"Earl!" Shelby glanced at Ashley apologetically before jogging over to Earl and Preston. "Come on now, Earl, you're going to talk Preston's ear off."

She dragged Earl away.

Finally, the round was ending. Shelby was exasperated and ready to strangle Earl, but she didn't because if she did, she'd be liable to getting court-martialed, and besides, he'd probably die from the poison-drug blow dart soon anyway. As the Harringtons were saying goodbye, Ashley slipped a note into Shelby's palm.

* * *

"Yes, a suit, Earl." Shelby wasn't happy because Earl wasn't happy because she'd taken him out shopping. The note Ashley Harrington had slipped Shelby at the golf course invited them to dinner at the Diamond Cubano Restaurante, and since it sounded like a fancy place, Shelby didn't want her and Earl to come off as rubes. Earl looked nice in a Seersucker blue- and white-striped suit, pink shirt and navy bow tie. And Shelby liked the off-the-

OOPS-A-NAVY

shoulder silver sequin lace gown she'd purchased. Sure, Bull Gompers would hit the ceiling when she saw three grand on their expense account, but the Harringtons could be the key to finding Senator Canfield, especially with what Ashley had said about them wanting to find him too. You had to pay for first-class intel.

Shelby and Earl showered in the De La Rata clubhouse locker room, donned their exclusive duds and were ready. A bicycle taxi—driven by Manuel, a friendly little Cuban pedaler with a handlebar mustache—was fortuitously waiting right outside the door, so they jumped into its sidecar and off they went to the restaurant.

In five minutes flat, Manuel pulled up in front of the Diamond Cubano. "Here you are. That'll be eighty-five US dollars."

"What?!" It was as if Earl came alive. "That's crazy! For a five-minute ride!"

Manuel shrugged. He lit a cigar. "Union rules. We've got minimums."

Earl frowned and reluctantly forked over the money. As they walked up the restaurant steps, he said to Shelby, "Good thing the Navy is paying for all this."

"How 'bout it?" Shelby, thinking maybe she was showing a little too much cleavage, pulled up her gown. (She was from Kansas after all.) When they walked into the restaurant, she just stood there staring. "Earl, could there be *another* Diamond Cubano Restaurante? Because this place is a dump."

The restaurant had a faux-corrugated tin roof, industrial-sized lighting fixtures hanging from it. A chalkboard leaning on one wall listed "Eats," half of the board devoted to "Carne," the other half to "Veggie." A bar with twenty-somethings sitting at it accounted for half of the restaurant. A sign over the bar read, "Think interesting thoughts."

Shelby, afraid of being under-dressed, now felt woefully

over-dressed and thought no interesting thoughts whatsoever.

The people sitting at the bar gawked as Shelby and Earl walked by. A beatnik-type with a denim backpack draped over his bar stool said, "Where's the wedding?"

Shelby thought about scissor kicking the punk, but it would've been difficult in the gown so she walked on. In a corner booth sat Ashley Harrington. Shelby, Earl trailing, made a beeline for her.

"Oh my goodness!" Ashley stood and put a hand to her mouth. "Don't you two look splendid."

That made Shelby feel a little better, and Earl thought Ashley looked hot in her tube top and miniskirt, sunglasses perched on her head.

"Still." Shelby shrugged. "I'd say we're a little overdressed for this place."

"Oh." Ashley hugged her. "I'm sorry. I thought you knew the Cubano was a hipster hangout. But, darling, you look marvelous, and you know what they say, it's always better to be over than under-dressed."

Here it was again—that old rube feeling Shelby was so familiar with—feeling like she was from Kansas, which of course she was.

"I'd say you're looking pretty sharp yourself, Ashley." Earl ogled her and was secretly glad Preston wasn't around.

"Why, thank you, kind sir." Ashley curtsied and sat. "Well, come have a seat. Preston had to have an emergency Upper GI and couldn't make it."

"I've had one of those," Earl said, sliding in next to her. "Too much stress." He scoped her again and added, "You are one hot blonde."

"Earl!" Shelby sat and wondered if it was the poison-drug blow dart talking or just his normal out-of-control horniness.

"No, Shelby. That's okay. I'm flattered." Ashley winked at

OOPS-A-NAVY

her. "Oh, here's our waiter. And we must have drinks. May I suggest the banana daiquiris, and let's get them with a scoop of vanilla ice cream on top, okay?"

"I'm game." Earl unbuttoned his suit coat.

Shelby wasn't so sure Earl should be drinking on top of the poison-drug blow dart, but the banana daiquiris with the ice cream did sound good. She looked up at the hunky waiter. He wore a black dago-T, biceps bulging. She smiled at him. "Sure, why not."

The waiter returned her smile and was off.

Shelby was wondering how to ease into a conversation about Senator Canfield when Ashley said, "I hope you don't mind, but I really wanted to talk about Senator Canfield for a bit."

"Oh?" Shelby leaned back in the booth.

"Is that all right?"

"Well, of course it is, Ashley. And actually we'd like to talk about him too."

The drinks arrived. Earl, not wanting to mess with the ice cream, asked for a straw.

Ashley smiled at him. He crept even closer. While Shelby was getting ready to kick him under the table.

Ashley adjusted her tube top. "I have to tell you, though, I'm concerned about talking to you about him. There are so many communist spies on the island, and when you said you were looking for the senator too, but that you were both dentists, I wondered how you could find the time."

Earl sat silently but Shelby kicked him anyway. "Ashley, Earl and I are charter members of Dentists With*in* Borders, which has flex time now—other dentists back home in Cleveland are covering for us."

"Ok." Ashley playfully pushed Earl away a bit. "I just wanted to make sure you were legit."

Shelby downed her banana daiquiri in one shot, a vanilla ice cream mustache on her lip. "Oh, we're legit all right."

As the night went on, the banana daiquiris flowed like, well, like banana daiquiris. Shelby was concerned about them getting too drunk, but she figured the bananas had a moderating effect. Anyway, they forgot to order dinner. And now Earl had his arm around Ashley, and Shelby would've kicked him again, but she was entranced with their waiter. Giorgio, he'd said his name was.

However, when Shelby went to the bathroom and finally remembered their mission, she decided it was time to call a taxi and get out of there before something bad happened. She was happy to hear that the bicycle-taxi driver that drove them before, Manuel, was still on duty, and he said he could be there in ten minutes. "Good enough," Shelby told him, and then she washed her hands and went back into the restaurant.

Only to find that Earl and Ashley were gone.

Chapter Six

"Oh boy," Shelby mumbled, standing at their table scattered with empty banana daiquiri glasses. What a mess, she thought. But deeper things than the messy table troubled her. Earl was gone. And so was Ashley. Not that she cared that much about either of them, but she cut Earl a little slack anyway because of the poison-drug blow dart. But yeah, it was mildly troubling that Ashley was gone too because Shelby was starting to like her. Although all the banana daiquiris may have had something to do with that.

Giorgio came up from behind and slipped his arms around her waist.

"Yes, Giorgio?"

"You are so sexy in this gown. Please forgive me, pretty American lady, but I just had to give you a hug."

Giorgio was a hunk, yes, but what about Earl being missing? Didn't she have a responsibility for finding him? She turned to Giorgio, and he kissed her on the lips! "Easy, big boy," she said. "You're one heck of an *hombre* for sure, and I do appreciate your physical charms, but I've a duty to find my compatriot first."

Giorgio shrugged. "Ah, that guy was a chump. You're better off without him."

Shelby slapped him. Where did that come from? Even though Earl really was a chump, she wasn't letting him be insulted.

"I like that." Giorgio rubbed his cheek. "A woman with fire in her veins."

"Yes, Giorgio." She wrinkled her nose. "Wasn't there a movie named that?"

"I think so, but I didn't see it."

"Anyway, yes, Giorgio, I've fire in my veins, and you best watch out lest you get burned."

"Ha ha. I'm not afraid of you, *gringa*." He looked at the table strewn with the empty banana daiquiri glasses. He pulled the bill from his waiter's apron and looked at it. "*Ay caramba!*"

"What's the damage?"

"Seven hundred and sixty-three US dollars."

"You sure it's not pesos?"

"Positive."

Shelby thought of Bull Gompers again. When Bull got their expense account she'd have a stroke. But whatever. "That's a little high, I'd say, for just a few drinks."

He gave her a sexy Cuban stare. "I could do a little creative figuring if you'd come home with me."

She glared at him, thinking she wasn't joining the cavalcade of #metoo sexual harassment victims. Although his offer was tempting. "Er, I don't think so, Giorgio." She handed him the American Express card.

"We don't take American Express."

Shelby shrugged. "Well, that's all I've got."

Manuel walked in. "Did anybody request a bicycle taxi?"

"In here, Manuel!" Shelby called. Meanwhile, Giorgio peered at her with violent lust in his eyes.

The little Cuban bicycle-taxi driver came to their booth. "Well, let's go. You're my last fare for the night."

Giorgio stared him down. "The gringa's not going anywhere."

"Hey," Shelby said, cracking her knuckles. "I didn't know you didn't take American Express. You should've had a sign on the door. I'll give you my address in Kansas. You can send me the bill."

"No can do, gringa."

"Quit calling me that, will you? Whatever it means, the way you're saying it sounds offensive."

"I don't care how it sounds. You're not leaving without

paying. Paying with money—or with your lovely body."

"Look, before I kill you, you better get the manager."

"What about me?" Manuel was standing there, twirling the ends of his mustache. "I came all the way out here in the middle of the night and need to get paid."

The hunky waiter sauntered off.

Shelby grabbed the little complaining Cuban bicycle-taxi driver. "Let's get out of here, Manuel!"

They ran for the door. Outside, they jumped onto the bicycle taxi, Shelby drunk, misjudging her leap and landing on her hip. "Go go go!"

Giorgio burst out of the restaurant and sprinted after them.

"Faster, faster!" Shelby yelled. She wished she had a riding crop—like her grandpa Chester in Kansas gave her—to whack Manuel with. Of course she could always just slap him, but that didn't seem appropriate somehow as it was late and she *was* his last fare. But the end result was—without inflicting violence on the little bicycle-taxi driver—Giorgio was gaining on them.

"Well, it's hard pedaling for two, especially as you're hardly a featherweight," Manuel squawked.

Now Shelby figured—appropriate or not—she'd smack him, but she had a bigger problem because Giorgio leaped into the sidecar with her.

Shelby was used to hand-to-hand combat but not with sexy Cuban waiters. And, truth be told, it wasn't unpleasant tussling with the hunk. After all, he wasn't *that* dangerous, and she'd really liked the compliment he'd paid her about being a "pretty American lady" and the sexy, bold hug and kiss he'd given her back in the restaurant. But when all was said and done, she *was* from Kansas and had morals. No, it was time to clean the big fella's clock. "You're messing with the wrong gringa, big boy!"

"Oh yeah?!"

Manuel looked at Shelby. "Get him off of here, will you? It's hard enough pedaling you."

"Hear that, Giorgio?" Shelby karate chopped him and twisted his arm behind his back. "You're extra weight on this gravy train."

"If you don't get rid of him, I'm stopping pedaling." Manuel sounded serious. "I'll have a heart attack moving all this tonnage."

Well, Shelby thought, "tonnage" was an unfair exaggeration, but it *was* time to cut loverboy loose. "You need to learn respect for women, Giorgio. I hope you'll remember this the next time you sexually harass someone."

"You are one tough broad, gringa. I love it." Giorgio tried to kiss her, but before he could, Shelby broke his arm and dumped him from the sidecar.

"Finally," Manuel said.

Before long, Shelby realized Manuel was taking her to De La Rata Country Club when she really needed to go to her tent in the jungle, where hopefully Earl would be. Oh boy, Manuel was not going to be happy about bicycling her to the jungle, especially since the jungle terrain was rough, it was late and she *was* his last fare of the day. She would break it to him gently.

"Manuel, you saved me back there at the restaurant." She reached out and squeezed his shoulder. (She was glad she hadn't smacked him.)

"That's true," he said, "but don't touch me, okay? Passengers aren't allowed to touch bicycle-taxi drivers. It's in our union rules. Besides, you're really drunk."

Well, Shelby thought, she *was* really drunk, and she kind of liked that Manuel was a man of morals, a man of integrity. Oh well, no more beating around the bush. "Manuel, I need you to take me to the jungle."

Manuel scoffed. "Geez, all you horny American broads think you can have your way with us Cubans. I'm *not* having sex with

OOPS-A-NAVY

you!"

Shelby realized Manuel had taken what she'd said as the figurative jungle. "No, no, you've got it all wrong, Manuel. I meant *literally* the jungle."

"Oh." He kept pedaling. He seemed to be thinking. "So then you're saying you *don't* want to have sex?"

"No!"

"No?"

"I mean, yes."

"Oh."

"Why?"

He curled one side of his mustache. "Well, because I was kind of flattered you wanted to. So you're not really attracted to me, then?"

"No, no, Manuel." She felt bad and touched his shoulder again, and this time he didn't complain. "I think you're very attractive for a little minority fellow, and I'm especially attracted to you because of your high morals and integrity."

"But not attracted enough to have sex?"

Shelby shrugged. He was kind of cute in his little third-world way. But no, that was the banana daiquiris talking. And she was from Kansas, after all. "Well, I'm not saying I'd *never* want to have sex with you, but come on, we hardly know each other."

Manuel nodded. "Well, that's true. But I'm really tired and don't feel like pedaling anymore."

"Ah, come on, it's not that far. And if I wasn't so drunk I'd help you pedal."

"Well, I guess it's okay then." He turned and headed for the jungle.

When they finally reached the tent, Manuel was huffing and puffing so, and with Earl not being there and his side of the tent open, Shelby could hardly send him back on his own. "Manuel, you can stay with me tonight, but no monkey business, and then pedal back in the morning."

"You're staying in a tent? In the jungle? That doesn't sound too safe."

What could she say to that? Should she tell him she was a SEAL? She was so tired and drunk she decided to go for it. "Manuel, you'll be safe with me. I'm a SEAL."

"Seal, like the fish?"

Shelby took a deep breath and sighed it out. "No, Manuel—and seals aren't fish, they're marine mammals—I'm a highly trained American military warrior."

"Why do they call you a seal, then? Why not tiger or wolf? Seals are fat and lazy and just lie around on rocks all day."

"Manuel." He was causing such a hassle she almost wanted to take her invitation back. "Just trust me. You'll be safe."

He stroked his mustache for quite a while. "Okay, I'll stay. And we won't have sex. But you think I'm attractive enough to, right?"

"Absolutely."

"I just say that because your suddenly not wanting to was messing with my self-esteem."

"No, Manuel, I think you're *mucho macho*."

"Oh, I like that—you know some Spanish."

* * *

Shelby clearly pointed out Manuel's side of the tent. She wished she'd had a magic marker to make it even clearer, but she thought he understood.

"Do you have any tortillas? After all that pedaling, I'm kind of hungry." Manuel settled down on Earl's side and was paging through one of his notebooks.

Shelby wondered if Earl would be upset Manuel was touching his stuff, but that was part of the Navy SEAL Code of

OOPS-A-NAVY

Ethics too—be kind to little people. Of course they may have meant that figuratively but whatever. Manuel was little in both ways.

"No tortillas, Manuel, but we have SPAM and Oatmeal."

"Okay, the SPAM sounds good."

She perused their SPAM collection. Well, he was a Cuban, so she grabbed a can of Jalapeño SPAM. She opened it, stuck a plastic fork in it and handed it to him. "You're gonna love it."

He took a bite. "Oh, that's pretty hot."

She tossed him a bottle of water. "You'll get used to it."

He gulped the water, not a little dribbling down his chin. "Yeah, okay."

Shelby sat cross-legged on the buoyant tent floor. "So, that was pretty unusual what happened with Giorgio back at the restaurant?"

Manuel took another bite of SPAM and followed it quickly with the water. "Not really. A lot of Cubans chase American women. They're looking to marry them so they can get a green card."

"They want to get off the island—get away from the scourge of communism?"

"Nah, they just don't want to work. Cubans are pretty poor and lazy. Like me. You think I want to be a bicycle-taxi pedaler my whole life? No, we'd rather marry a rich American broad and do nothing."

Shelby shrugged. "But you manage to make a living obviously."

"Only because of rich tourists. I just hang around the golf course and sooner or later somebody always needs a ride."

"At least it's good honest work."

"Yeah, thanks, but would you want to do it?"

"Well, now that you put it that way." She took off her shoes and massaged her feet.

51

Manuel set the SPAM on the tent floor. "I can do that for you if you want."

Shelby loved getting foot rubs. "Really?"

"Sure, as long as you don't have athlete's foot or that toenail fungus."

Shelby smiled. "Okay."

"You don't have athlete's foot?"

"No."

"Or the toenail fungus?"

"No, I don't have that either."

He came to her side of the tent, sat and took one of her feet into his lap. "My ex-wife said I was really good at this." He kneaded her foot.

"So you were married?"

"Uh, not really."

"Well, why did you say you had an ex-wife?"

"Well, we almost got married."

"Ok." Shelby laughed. "And as long as we're making true confessions, I should tell you I'm from Kansas."

"Never heard of it." He slipped off her sock.

"Now hold on a minute, Manuel. I didn't say you could do that." But there was a thrill of having it come off, and Manuel was good to his word that he was a gifted foot masseuse.

"I can put it back on. I can just massage it better without my hands slipping across the sock."

Shelby had no reason not to believe him as her socks *were* slippery. "Okay, but remember, if you try anything funny, I'm a SEAL."

"You keep saying that." He slipped off her other sock. "I think it's kind of strange."

As he massaged, Shelby, luxuriating, leaned back, closed her eyes and felt as if she went to a different spot on the space-time continuum. "Oh, that feels soooo good."

OOPS-A-NAVY

"I knew you'd like it without the socks."

"So, Giorgio—"

"What, I'm Manuel." He stopped massaging.

"Oh, my bad. No, please keep going. So, Manuel, you know how when you picked me up the first time I was with a man? But when you picked me up the second time I was alone?"

"No, I don't remember that but go on." He resumed massaging.

"Well, yeah, the first time there was a guy."

"So what happened to him?"

"That's the thing. I don't know. It was at the restaurant. He was with another woman when I last saw him. I went to the bathroom and when I came out, they were gone."

"So he was like kidnapped?" He stopped massaging again. "My hands are getting tired."

"Oh, okay." Shelby put her socks back on. "I don't know. What do you think?"

"Well, a lot of wealthy Americans get kidnapped by Cubans for ransom. Like I said, most of us are really poor and looking for easy money."

Shelby shook her head. "But the woman he was with *was* American."

"Ah." Manuel yawned. "Excuse me." He looked Shelby in the eye. "Then she was probably a spy. Cuba is crawling with CIA spies."

Chapter Seven

What Manuel said about Ashley being a spy stuck with Shelby, and that night she dreamt she was in a James Bond movie. Only thing was, *she* was the villain. In the morning, she woke up troubled. She looked across the tent expecting to see Earl and hear his early morning flatulence, but instead, Manuel was sitting there eating another can of Jalapeño SPAM.

"I hope it's okay I took this. I've come to really love the stuff." Manuel picked his teeth with the plastic fork. "You know, I really have to get back to work though."

Shelby thought about asking him for another foot rub but passed on the idea—Earl was out there somewhere, and if he hadn't died yet, she had a responsibility to at least make a token effort to find him. Especially if he'd been kidnapped by Ashley, the probable spy.

They zipped up the tent and headed out on the bicycle taxi. As they were driving by De La Rata Golf Course, Shelby saw Ashley and Earl playing the seventh hole—a sign said the hole was named Large Chameleon—which ran right along the ocean. Oh, all the greenery, it was such a beautiful sight, and the sound of the waves crashing on the beach only made it more enjoyable. But duty called. Shelby told Manuel to stop pedaling and wait for her. She ran out onto the course.

"Ashley! Earl!"

Earl hit a shot and looked at Shelby. "Hi!"

Shelby was standoffish with Ashley, especially considering that Ashley might've kidnapped Earl, and because Manuel said she was a spy. "Ashley, what happened to you two last night?"

"Oh." Ashley looked at Earl as if trying to draw her answer out of him. "Well, while we were waiting for you to come back

OOPS-A-NAVY

from the restroom, Giorgio came to our table and said there was a bomb threat and we needed to leave right away. So we went out into the night and started running, then got lost."

Manuel came walking up. "How long do you expect me to wait? I gave you a foot rub, okay, but that doesn't mean I'm your slave."

Earl jammed a nine-iron into his golf bag. "He gave you a foot rub?! Who is this guy, Shelby? What happened last night between you two?"

"He's just Manuel." Shelby shrunk back, but then gathered herself. "Wait a minute! You two are dodging my questions. You just went running out into the night? And didn't think to come back for me?"

Manuel sidled up to her and whispered in her ear. "I told you she's probably a spy."

"Hey, fella." Earl walked over to the diminutive Cuban. "I don't like you whispering in Shelby's ear." He lifted Manuel onto his shoulders, twirled him around a few times, then body-slammed him into a sand trap.

Shelby gave Earl a high five. "Cool move, Earl! It reminded me of a WWF match when Hulk Hogan did that to Dusty Spartan and killed him."

"Oh my God. That was so uncalled-for." Ashley had tears in her eyes.

Manuel dragged himself out of the sand trap, sand mashed into his mustache. "Yes, it definitely wasn't called for. I'm leaving."

"Oh, Manuel, it was only in the sand." Shelby brushed him off as he walked to his bicycle taxi. "And earlier, you got to enjoy some SPAM."

"Yeah, that part was good," Manuel acknowledged before pedaling off.

Earl and Ashley climbed back into their golf cart.

Shelby threw up her hands. "No! No more golf until we straighten this out!"

Earl tugged on his earlobe. "Well, we gotta keep up. There are golfers behind us."

"No, you don't." Shelby climbed into the golf cart, sliding Earl over, knocking Ashley off.

"What about Ashley?" Earl said as Shelby hit the gas and they sped away.

"She'll be okay. But, Earl, I've got big news for you—she's a spy."

"Don't say that, Shelby."

"But she is. Manuel told me."

"Manuel, the little beaner I just body-slammed into the sand trap?"

"Yeah."

"How would he know?"

"Earl, okay, he's a poor lazy Cuban, but he's also a man of high morals and integrity. I trust him."

"Yeah, you trusted him enough to give you a foot rub. Did he give you anything else?"

"Wow. Talk about uncalled-for." Shelby cut across a fairway and golfers yelled at them, a golf ball bouncing off the roof of their cart.

"No, Shelby. You discouraging me whenever I fall for someone is what's uncalled-for. You always do this."

"Earl, she's a spy!"

"Yeah? So what?"

"So what?! We're here to rescue Senator Canfield. And you have to remember you still have the blow dart poison drug in your system. You don't want to be making any major decisions while under its influence."

They pulled into the country club parking lot, and the golf cart's tires squealed as Shelby braked hard.

OOPS-A-NAVY

"Well." Earl wiped the sweat from his forearms. He was a little concerned, though, that he was removing sunscreen too and that he'd have to re-apply it. "You know what, I think you may be right. I did find myself doing some strange things with Ashley last night."

"I don't want to hear about it."

"Well, who else am I going to tell?"

"Bull Gompers."

"Funny."

"Seriously, Earl, we need to stay on mission."

"And you?" Earl climbed from the golf cart. "You've stayed on mission, getting foot rubs from the Cuban homunculus?"

"What's a homunculus?"

"The shrimp bicycle-taxi guy!"

"He wasn't *that* small."

"But you stayed on mission?"

"Let's drop it, Earl. I'll call a taxi because we need a ride to Guantanamo. From there we can radio Bull Gompers and see if Navy intel has anything for us regarding Senator Canfield. But yeah, we need to stay on mission, okay?" She walked around the golf cart and offered him the Navy SEAL handshake.

Earl seemed to get pumped when he saw it. He slapped his hand into hers. "SEALs forever, Shelby!"

"SEALs forever!" she replied, but she was convinced he was still out of his mind. She called the taxi company.

* * *

"Oh no, not you two again." When Manuel pulled up to the golf course and saw Shelby and Earl, he started pedaling off.

Shelby ran after him. "Manuel, give us another chance."

"No thanks," he called over his shoulder.

Shelby caught the escaping little Cuban. "There. I got you."

Earl joined them.

Shelby said, "Manuel, let's clear the air, okay? It's only right. Especially considering what happened was mostly your fault."

"My fault! How was it my fault?"

"I said 'mostly,' Manuel. Now come on. Let's start over."

"Not with the psycho." He nodded toward Earl. "I've got to protect my self-esteem, you know."

Shelby turned to her fellow SEAL. "Earl, apologize."

Earl shrugged. "For what?"

"For body-slamming me into the sand trap," Manuel snapped.

"That still bothering you?"

"Earl." Shelby grabbed his bad arm.

"Ow!"

"Just do it."

Earl rolled his neck. "Sure. Sorry, beaner."

Manuel stared off into space. "That really hurt, you know. I think my kidneys are bruised."

"Yeah, I knew it might rough you up a bit." Earl patted the little Cuban's head. "But that's why I did it in the sand. I knew it wouldn't kill you there."

"Oh, okay." Manuel ventured to look Earl in the eye. "That at least makes me feel a little better."

"So we're all good now?" Shelby smiled. "Can you two shake?"

Earl offered his hand and Manuel slowly took it. Then Manuel drove them to Guantanamo.

*   *   *

At Guantanamo, Shelby and Earl were shown the usual deferential respect and utter contempt. Respect because SEALs were superior warriors. Contempt because the Army, Marines, Air

OOPS-A-NAVY

Force and Coast Guard personnel stationed on the base knew that. Not surprisingly, the base commander said he had no new intel on Senator Canfield's disappearance. Still, with all the inter-services' jealousy and backbiting going on, Shelby knew he might have something, and he just wasn't sharing it. They commandeered a secure radio and called Bull Gompers.

"Admiral Gompers," Shelby said. "Can you hear me?"

"Of course I can, Ryder. I'm not deaf."

"It's good to hear your voice, ma'am," Earl said.

"Spare me the small talk, you two, and tell me what actionable intelligence you've come up with on Senator Canfield."

Earl scratched his head. "Uh…"

"That's what I thought." Bull laughed bitterly.

Shelby spoke up. "We have made some profitable contacts. We met two Americans who had Senator Canfield as a member of their golf foursome, and they're looking for him as well."

"That's it?" The irritation in Bull's tone of voice was obvious.

"We met a Cuban homunculus." Earl thought it couldn't hurt to mention Manuel.

"A what?"

Shelby jumped in. "Admiral, SEAL Bernstein was hit by a poison-drug blow dart in the jungle and hasn't been himself lately."

"Well, that can only be an improvement," Bull said. "All right now, listen up, you two, because this is important. Navy SEAL high command has received intelligence from an asset we think is credible. The intelligence suggests that Senator Canfield is being held in a remote area, heavily subject to Commie influence, all the way on the other side of the island called Candlebrake Cove—"

"Ah," Shelby interjected. "That's why we couldn't find him

here!"

"Ryder, interrupt me again, and I'll have you thrown in the cells with the jihadists there at Guantanamo."

"Sorry, ma'am."

"And now, I want you both to pay extra special attention because what I'm about to tell you has earth-shattering implications." She paused. "This mission is no longer about just Senator Canfield being missing. International tensions are escalating. The president's tweeted he's sure the Russians are behind the senator's disappearance and that he has his finger poised over the nuclear button. So the fact of the matter is, if you don't get Canfield back soon, the nukes are gonna fly. Yes, we're talking the end of the world."

"Admiral." Shelby had a tear in her eye and sniffled. "I'm touched by your confidence in us to accomplish this grave mission."

"Yeah, well, it was just because I couldn't find anybody else. Now go back to your tent, and a helicopter will drop a rope basket to you in the morning and then fly you to the other side of the island, where you can parachute into the cove."

Chapter Eight

Morning came around quickly. Shelby reflected on the time they'd spent there in the jungle. It had been hard, with the boa constrictor crushing her leg and Earl being out of his fricking mind from the poison-drug blow dart, but she'd miss it. And she'd miss Giorgio and even diminutive Manuel. Giorgio for his sheer animal magnetism and Manuel because, although lazy and opportunistic, he was eminently decent and of high moral character. Earl seemed heartbroken to be leaving Ashley, but Shelby reminded him Ashley was a spy and that he'd be better off without her.

They packed up their gear, then waited for the helicopter. They could hear the helicopter's thudding rotors well before they saw anything, and then they felt the rush of wind, the palm tree fronds bending like in a hurricane, the underbrush swirling, dust and lizards being kicked up everywhere. Then finally a massive blue two-rotor helicopter appeared. It was a sight for sore eyes, and Shelby and Earl experienced a rush of patriotism and felt renewed confidence as to why they'd dedicated their lives to killing people for the government. "NAVY" was emblazoned on the chopper in white, and next to it was the five-point Navy star. They got emotional and weepy looking on. Then a door opened and a basket attached to a drop line shot down in measured swoops.

Shelby, thinking Earl might still be insane from the poison-drug blow dart and harboring intentions of staying behind because of Ashley, made him climb into the basket first. Next was her turn. She felt wistful gazing down at their base camp as the basket rose. It was always difficult leaving places, but she knew in her heart that they'd been hugely successful here, and now they were off to even bigger successes.

Taking advantage of the downtime, they both slept on the flight. They were woken five minutes before the jump. They checked their parachutes. They were ready. But looking down, they realized Candlebrake Cove was not all that big and the water was surrounded by mountains with sharp rock outcroppings.

Shelby grabbed a headset and said to the helicopter pilot, "Can't you drop us somewhere with fewer rocks?"

"No can do, SEAL," came the voice back. "These were my orders. It's either drop here or abort."

Shelby was not going to abort a mission in progress. She'd been trained to die instead. "You ready, Earl?"

Earl's eyes betrayed his terror. Shelby helped him stand and coaxed him to the open door. The ocean farther out was dark blue, white lines of breakers pushing into the shoals of brown seaweed ringing the shore, but the cove water was green and calm. The problem was the surrounding rocks, which looked razor sharp, and one towering boulder protruding from the middle of the water.

They got a nod from the crew and a thumbs-up.

Shelby gave Earl a gentle smile. "Ready, SEAL?"

"Actually, I'm feeling a bit queasy."

Shelby knew they had to jump. "I'll go first. Then you follow me, okay?"

He nodded.

Shelby waved to the helicopter crew, pushed Earl out and then jumped.

As they fell, Shelby got Earl a goodly enough distance from her so their chutes wouldn't tangle. Closer to the water, Shelby could see the cove was gorgeous, inviting, pristine, not a soul on the beach. She was surprised such a beautiful place would be empty, but then again, there were the surrounding mountains isolating it from the rest of the island.

OOPS-A-NAVY

She gave Earl a thumbs-up. Yeah, okay, he looked unhappy, probably because she'd pushed him, but he was still not himself from the poison-drug blow dart. He might snap out of it, though. If he didn't die. They yanked their ripcords and their chutes deployed.

Shelby pulled her steering rein to the left and headed toward the shore, but Earl was caught in the trade winds and would soon be blowing over the rock outcroppings. Her only hope of saving him was getting him to jettison his chute before he got over the rocks. He'd land in the cove but being in open water was second nature to a SEAL.

"Jettison the chute!" Shelby waved her arms to get his attention, and pantomiming the necessary motion, she accidentally jettisoned *her* chute. "Ahhhhhh!" She tried to use her Navy SEAL emergency training (basically, extending her arms like Superman) to guide herself away from the shore, but given the aerodynamics of the situation there was only so much she could do. She checked on Earl, and he at least had taken the hint and jettisoned his chute and was also plummeting, but safely over deeper water. Shelby pressed her legs together and held her arms tightly to her sides. This was going to hurt! A few more nanoseconds and then…

Splashdown!

She'd managed to hit the water instead of the beach, but it was relatively shallow water, and her feet got stuck in the sand. Except for her hands, she was fully submerged, and she could see Earl landing safely farther out in the cove. Meanwhile, she was really stuck and struggling to get free and that meant she was rapidly using up her very limited supply of oxygen. She would've called to Earl for help but she was underwater. She gestured frantically to him with her hands, though, but he was doing the backstroke (his favorite stroke) on his way to shore and didn't see.

Shelby was a goner. She remembered her dead parents and breathed her last. Just then she saw a glowing white light at the end of a tunnel or really it was more of a corridor, like in a warehouse, and she heard her childhood friend Abigail saying that Shelby hadn't returned her Malibu Barbie (Malibu Barbie was big in Kansas because the state was so far from the ocean). What she was seeing was so beautiful, Shelby thought, except she was sure she'd returned the Barbie, but even so, she wanted to go down the corridor to the light. If this was death, she wasn't complaining. She released herself to the experience.

But wait! A voice told her she wasn't done on earth yet! That the universe still had something for her to do, at least for a few more months. Well, Shelby thought, if it was only for a few more months she might as well go to the light now. Who knew if she'd get another chance? But the voice was insistent. Like your dental office reminding you of your appointment for a cleaning. She was needed. Then she felt strong arms encircle her and powerfully lift her from the sand, up above the surf.

"Earl?"

But it wasn't Earl. It was a vision! Well, maybe not a vision, but this guy was definitely not from Kansas. He was gorgeous. Tan, muscular, shirtless, with long curly black hair in a ponytail. He was clean-shaven and wore what looked to be a three-carat diamond in his left ear. Shelby had died and gone to heaven! "Are you an angel?"

"No, I am Hemana. I live in the cove." He carried her to the shore and laid her on the sand.

"He-man?"

"Heman*a*." He lay down beside her.

Well, he was a real he-man to her. "I'm Shelby." She looked down the beach and saw Earl writing in a notebook.

"I am from Samoa."

"I am from Kansas."

OOPS-A-NAVY

"I am grateful the universe has allowed for our convergence."

"Me, too, beautiful Samoan He-man."

"Heman*a*."

"Gotcha."

"I see you have a friend." Hemana nodded toward Earl.

"Yeah, Earl. Yeah, he's with me, I guess. But it's not like we're married or anything. In fact, he might be dead soon."

"You both fell from the big bird in the sky at the same time. Are the gods angry with you?"

Shelby laughed. She didn't think the gods had anything to do with it. "Not yet, I don't think. But if we screw up this mission, well, that's a different story."

"Mission?"

Should she tell him? Probably not, but he did save her life. Shelby was at the point where she needed to take really big chances. Her biological clock was ticking, after all. "We're looking for something."

"Aren't we all?" Hemana smiled comfortably. "You must come to The Gathering—he'd said it with such reverential respect—tonight and perhaps you will find what you are looking for."

That sounded all right to Shelby. And that would give her and Earl a chance to establish a base camp and get cleaned up. (She could feel she had kelp in her hair and sand in her thong.) She checked her Breitling Exospace B55 wristwatch. "What time?"

"We do not go by clock time here." Hemana stood. "We gather right before the sun eases into the ocean."

"Well, we'll see you then." Shelby smiled. The guy was a dream. Oh, he had a tattoo on his right shoulder running down his arm that might not go over well with her grandparents back in Kansas, but things were looking very good to say the least. She walked down the beach to Earl, who was still writing in a notebook.

He looked up. "I think this poem I just wrote is a real winner,

Shelby. I'm thinking of sending it to *The New Yorker*."

Shelby usually didn't want to hear his stupid poetry, but she was feeling so magnanimous after meeting Hemana she ran with the positive vibe. "Would you read it to me?"

"Okay, but remember I just wrote it, so it may need a tweak or two."

She nodded.

He rubbed his hands together. "*Falling from the sky / At first I thought I would die / I felt like the opposite of the Catcher in the Rye / And that if I were Neil Young I'd feel like getting high.*"

"Huh, it has a nice ring to it, Earl."

"I'm not done." He looked at the notebook. "*The spirit world deceived me / But the water it received me / My heart, my soul refreshed / As my parachute unmeshed.*"

"Wow."

"There's more. *True, Shelby pushed me / But even that didn't smoosh me / My poems to live another day / My skin the rocks did not flay.*"

Shelby shook her head appreciatively. "Yeah, that is a real winner, Earl."

"I know."

"So listen, we need to set up a base camp, check in with Bull Gompers, and then the locals are having a welcoming party at dusk that we're invited to. Sound good?"

"Yep. Sure does." He snapped his notebook shut. "I think I'm going to like this place."

* * *

"Yes, Admiral," Shelby said into the two-way secure radio. "We've landed, set up camp and now we're going to canvass the locals by attending a meet and greet."

"Ryder," Bull Gompers warned, "our intel says the Cove is

OOPS-A-NAVY

crawling with Russian spies."

"Admiral, we have as yet to see anyone but a friendly Samoan guy named Hemana. I know the 'a' on the end sounds weird but that's the guy's name."

"What the hell are you talking about, Ryder?"

"You're right, ma'am, I got off message there a bit."

"Is Bernstein okay? How's the blow dart affecting him?"

Shelby was tempted to say, "Believe it or not, his poetry seems to be improving" but knew that probably wouldn't play well. (Their mission wouldn't be gauged on the success of Earl's poetry.) "I'd say he's at 70%, ma'am."

"70% of that nut sounds dangerous as hell. Keep an eye on him, Ryder. You know what to do if he threatens the success of the mission."

Actually, Shelby didn't know, but how could she say that when Bull said she did? And what Bull said sounded ominous. Like if things weren't working out, she should give Earl a cyanide pill. Anyway, she took it as an okay to terminate him if he screwed up too much. Which was actually a welcome order. It clarified things and freed her up. "Absolutely, Admiral. Now it's sundown, and if it's okay with you, Earl and I need to go to the meet and greet. The intel we gather there should be highly actionable. We'll check back in with you soon."

"Ten-four, Ryder. Just remember if you and 70% don't come back with the senator, you're being de-SEALed *and* there will be a nuclear war."

"Roger that, Admiral." Shelby looked around for Earl. Where the heck did he go? "We won't let you down." She hung up the radio, unzipped the tent and stuck her head out. Earl was meditating in a little wooded area. He obviously wasn't worried about mosquitoes because he hadn't asked for the Lemon Eucalyptus spray, but now they had to hurry. "Earl, come on. The sun is almost down and we're going to be late for the meet and greet."

Earl jumped up and hurried to the tent. "What did Bull say?"

"She said we better get our rumps in gear and find the senator fast or we're getting de-SEALed *and* there'll be a nuclear war."

"Wow, it's hard to work under that kind of pressure."

"Agreed. But we're SEALs, Earl. We live for pressure."

Shelby crinkled her nose when she saw Earl putting on the Seersucker suit he'd worn to the Diamond Cubano Restaurante. "It'll be more casual tonight, Earl. We're going to want to blend in, not look like Southern Plantation owners. Just shorts and a T-shirt will do."

Earl changed and they were ready. They headed to the beach.

When they got there, Shelby said, "Oh my God, Earl, would you look at that!"

The sky was an immense canvas of pink and orange reflecting on the calm cove waters, its waves little measured lines just barely lapping the shore. The rock outcropping in the middle of the cove stood in dark contrast to the shimmering water. Blue-gray clouds tinged with orange built on the ocean horizon like mountain ranges.

Earl stood still as a statue. "Well, you certainly don't see anything like this in Chicago. You know, my parents wanted me to be a proctologist. They said there was good money in it, and that way I could still live at home with them. It's at times like these I'm glad I didn't listen."

"What's a proctologist?"

"Never mind."

A bonfire was burning on the beach. The flames rose like apparitions, dancing, twisting and taking on whatever images Shelby's and Earl's imaginations assigned. The flames were ghosts. Tongues of fire. Monsters.

A group had gathered around the fire. They sat impassively staring at it as if it were a deity, an oracle.

OOPS-A-NAVY

Shelby knew Earl with the blow dart poison drug in him was hardly a paragon of sobriety, but she had to ask somebody. "This is kind of spooky, Earl. Is it just me or are you too waiting for *The Twilight Zone* music to start playing?"

"The atmosphere is definitely funky."

"What do you mean funky?"

"Just go with it, Shelby. Don't think like a Kansan for once in your life."

Shelby was proud to be from Kansas, and now that Earl was dissing her and her home state, she was considering carrying out Bull's option to terminate him. But then here came the he-man Samoan, Hemana. Still shirtless (did he ever wear a shirt?) he offered them a peaceful smile. "Welcome to The Gathering."

Shelby's spirit quivered. It wasn't exactly fear. It was more akin to the curiosity of being thrust into a situation she'd never dreamed she'd experience. "Is this a séance, Hemana?"

The hunky Samoan laughed. "No, but you *are* here on a special night."

Shelby kept staring at the scene with bulging eyes. "I'm starting to feel so much. The vibe is so powerful here. My knees are getting weak."

Hemana nodded. "Tonight is the harmonic convergence of the Second Great Awakening."

"I think I've heard of that." Earl arched his back. "Something like that happens in Sedona, Arizona, every year. It's healing."

"Sedona is no doubt a special place, Earl." Hemana took them both by the hand and led them to the fire. "But this is different. The ancient Aztec wisdom predicted the planets coming together in alignment which signifies the beginning of the final heaven cycle."

Shelby squeezed Hemana's hand. "Holy cow."

"Sit and meditate with us for peace in the universe." Hemana pointed to two open spots next to each other as the sun sank into the ocean and the orange of the sea slowly transformed into darkening gray like a carpet rolling out.

Shelby and Earl sat next to each other on the warm sand. Warm from the day's sun. Warm from the fire. Warm from the radiating cosmic energy.

Hemana started the meeting. "Friends of the Second Great Awakening, welcome, and welcome to our new friends, Shelby and Earl." His serene gaze fell upon them.

Shelby thought Hemana was such a stud and kind and mindful to boot. She was convinced he was the man for her. She gave him a little wave. "Thanks, He-man."

"Heman*a*."

"Dang. My bad. Hemana."

"No worries, sister Shelby, for tonight the harmonic convergence will negate all mistakes. It will destroy the artificial constraints that keep us separate from one another and restore the world to its original blissful primordial unity."

Earl thought that was a lot of adjectives in a row, but then he was back to checking out the women. Honestly, he wasn't thrilled with any of them. He'd been so stuck on Ashley Harrington, anybody else paled in comparison. But he was enjoying the warmth and crackle of the fire and the psychic buzz in the air. It reminded him of the spiritualist meetings his parents took him to at the University of Chicago when he was little. "Cool," he said just to say something.

Hemana raised his arms and looked to the heavens. "We welcome you, oh long-awaited beneficent power who transforms the world. Come. Awaken our sleeping consciousnesses with your eternal tranquility. May health abound eternally. May peace abound eternally…"

Shelby could feel herself relaxing as Hemana went on.

"…May abundance abound eternally…"

Five minutes later, the peace fell so heavily on the group that

OOPS-A-NAVY

Earl nodded out and fell backward into the sand. Shelby thought, good thing it was sand and not concrete, otherwise he would've had a cerebral hematoma, and she would have had to explain a dead-Earl to Bull Gompers. She considered leaving him there lying in the sand, though, because that way he wouldn't say anything stupid, but there was the social expectation from the others that she set him back up, so she did.

"And now…" Hemana raised a silver chalice. "… we honor the earth with this blessed libation from its precious bounty." He sipped from the chalice and passed it to the person next to him. The chalice went around.

When it got to Earl he examined it but didn't drink. "It looks like a milkshake, but what's in it?" Earl, even under the effect of the blow dart poison drug, was careful about what he put into his body.

Hemana seemed to sense Earl's hesitation. "It's a mushroom smoothie, friend."

"Oh, in that case." Earl took a goodly gulp. His mother had told him mushrooms were healthful for the digestive system (something Earl was very concerned about as his Aunt Shirley had gotten colitis when she turned 100, and he believed he too might have a genetic predisposition for eventually getting the disease). He passed the chalice to Shelby, who drank from it without taking her eyes off the dazzling Hemana.

Shelby lost track of time for a few minutes, and when she came to, everything seemed different. People's voices sounded like they came from deep within a well, echoey. The bonfire flames turned purple. The people sitting around the campfire rippled. One resembled a lizard. Another Santa. And a heavenly light emanated from Hemana's long curly hair. This was freaking amazing. Especially for somebody from Kansas. Now she was able to make out some of the talk. It was Hemana. His voice was like golden honey flowing through the air and easing into her ear canals.

"Now, brothers and sisters," he was saying, "to honor the coming together of the planets and the harmonic convergence let *us* come together, join hands, close our eyes and pray for world peace."

Shelby looked at Earl, and she knew it was him, but he seemed shorter and fatter, and he was wearing a sombrero—where did he get it?—but yeah, she knew it was him somehow, so she offered and he took her hand. To her left sat Rosalyn, a forty-something woman with hair the color of galvanized aluminum and wearing a baseball cap. She held a half-full case of Beck's beer on her lap, but intermittently, she looked like a young Princess Diana wearing a brunette wig. When she looked like Rosalyn again, Shelby swallowed and took her hand. And when she did, she felt a sense of connection to the universe she'd never before experienced, even growing up in Kansas. It was as if there was no difference between her and the world around her. Like she'd fallen into a vat of liquefied Hershey's Kisses. All was one. And sweet. In the background, Hemana spoke again in a heavenly voice.

"Friends, the harmonic convergence is upon you. Love now rules the universe and is the king of your hearts. It is your whole being. Feel its energy move through and in you. Then feel it as it spreads out from you. To the person next to you. To your loved ones, here and departed. To the community. Even planet-wide. Bringing together all people who have been torn asunder by differences of race, politics, religion and geography.

"And now, as you slowly return your consciousness to the world around you, imagine that you are on fire with this cosmic love. That you radiate its light everywhere, that it overwhelms you as it joins with others' lights in an all-encompassing connection of everything everywhere. Namaste."

When Shelby finally opened her eyes, the bonfire itself

OOPS-A-NAVY

seemed aflame with love. She looked at Earl, who was still short and fat but no longer wearing the sombrero, and she smiled and squeezed his hand. Then she turned to her left and realized she was holding Senator Canfield's hand.

Chapter Nine

Shelby looked at Earl, panic flashing through her entire body. But when she looked back to Senator Canfield it was only Rosalyn again, the half-full case of beer still on her lap. What the heck was going on here?

Hemana and others in the group now stood, and they were bowing to each other and embracing. Shelby was wondering if she was the only one who'd seen Senator Canfield. She turned to Earl. "Did you see that?"

"See what?"

"Well." Her brow furrowed. "Senator Canfield. He was sitting right next to me."

Earl shrugged. "No, I didn't, but I would've sworn Elvis was sitting next to *me*. He was telling me he'd found spiritual enlightenment through this group, and as a bonus it had helped him lose weight."

Shelby nodded. It was all finally making sense—they'd been drugged! The "blessed libation," the "mushroom smoothie," had been full of LSD or maybe worse. (If there was worse. Shelby was from Kansas after all.) But Senator Canfield had seemed *so real*. His perfectly tailored navy suit, the crisp white shirt with the blue- and gold diagonally-striped tie, the cuff links, the winning smile. She'd never encountered the power of drugs before, but yeah, for those few moments Senator Canfield had been real. Was it possible he *had been* there? "You're sure you didn't see him, Earl?"

"I don't know. I might have. The whole scene was pretty funky there for a while, and I was freaked out that I was talking to Elvis. (And he did look like he'd lost weight.)"

This was crazy, Shelby thought as Earl wandered off. They

OOPS-A-NAVY

needed to get back to reality and find the real Senator Canfield, not his ghost or aura or holograph. She looked at Hemana. Oh, he was such a good-looking man, standing there, the fire reflecting off his golden skin. He was like a god. But she needed to be SEAL-tough. "Hey, Hemana."

"Shelby, blessings from the eternal be imparted to you." He bowed to her.

"Yeah, thanks, but why did you drug Earl and me with that smoothie? It was very unsettling to us, and especially to me since I'm from Kansas."

"Ah, blessed sister, the smoothie was simply God's mushrooms from his verdant green earth."

"Well, all I know is I was out of my fricking mind there for a while. In fact, I thought I was holding Senator Canfield's hand."

Hemana looked at her with a gaze of supreme lovingkindness. "How do you know you weren't?"

Just then Earl called to her. "Shelby, hurry, I just saw him!"

* * *

This was madness. Shelby ran to join Earl, who was standing at the edge of the cove. He was looking up into the rock outcroppings.

She asked, "You just saw *who*?"

"Senator Canfield!"

"No way." She looked up at the rocks. With the sun nearly down, the rocks were really dark now and looked menacing. "Where?"

He pointed. "He ran through that grove of palm trees, then scrambled up into the rocks."

"Well, how did you know it was him?"

"Sheesh, Shelby, I know what Senator Canfield looks like." He kept staring up at the rocks.

"Okay, what was he wearing?"

"What?"

"What was Senator Canfield wearing? Was he in cutoffs, a T-shirt and sandals?"

"No, no, he wore a business suit."

"What color?"

"Navy blue with a white shirt and a blue- and gold diagonally-striped tie."

Shelby had to sit down. Oh my God. What was happening here? "Are you sure it wasn't somebody else? A banker? A funeral parlor director? A Mormon missionary?"

"Shelby, I saw his face. What the hell."

Okay, Earl was only 70%, but he was making sense now. Shelby pulled out her phone. "Are mushrooms drugs?" she asked it.

She read a post. "Earl, they're called *magic* mushrooms. They're hallucinogenic *drugs*."

"Well, okay." He joined her sitting in the sand. "That would explain Elvis but what about seeing Senator Canfield?"

"You're right. I guess that really could've been the senator, but Earl..." Her words trailed off.

"What?"

Shelby was doing some deep thinking. "Things really are peaceful here in the cove, aren't they?" She looked around for Hemana, the man-a of her dreams.

Earl leaned forward. "Yeah, they sure are, Shelby, and it's really beautiful too, even prettier than Hawaii. I could write some epic poems here."

"But what do you make of all that eternal love and cosmic consciousness stuff?" As soon as she asked, she wondered if she really should be asking Earl, the victim of the poison-drug blow dart attack, and now with the hallucinogens floating through his system, he was no doubt even more seriously mentally impaired.

But whatever. She had no one else to ask.

"Well, for a while there I thought not only was Elvis sitting next to me but that he'd also become Hemana, and that he was conducting the rest of the group, which had turned into a German tuba band, so that wasn't all that peaceful and loving. But as Elvis transformed back into Hemana, and Hemana prayed or whatever he was doing, I felt like the blood flowing through my veins was a crystalline diamond stream."

"Wow, that's really neat, Earl." He's wasted.

"Yeah." He pushed out his chest. "Shelby, I actually feel like I'm getting in touch with my god-nature."

Being from Kansas, Shelby was tempted to scoff at that, but truth be told, she felt the same thing. "I know what you're saying, Earl. I feel pretty supernaturally powerful myself."

"I feel omnipotent."

"I wouldn't go that far."

"Yeah, you're right."

"But I think we have been enlightened. Don't you? Like we've attained our Buddha-natures."

Earl's gaze was fixed on her. "Namaste, Shelby."

"Namaste, Earl."

They nodded to each other and conked heads.

When they stopped seeing stars, Shelby said, "Can I give you a cosmic hug?"

"I was hoping you would say that." He opened his arms.

"Namaste," they said simultaneously one last time as they hugged and their spirits soared.

Chapter Ten

Next morning Shelby woke in Earl's arms. Her first thought was to strike him forcefully in the face, but as the memory of yesterday's cosmic peace washed over her she desisted. She knew that even though they had attained their Buddha-natures, not only did Earl remain the horniest guy who ever lived but also that she and he weren't happening romantically no matter how amazing the cosmic convergence had been. "Earl, move. You're crushing my pelvis."

He groaned and rolled off. "Namaste."

"Namaste, yourself!" No, this Buddha-nature mystic-wonder stuff would no longer do. They were SEALs for Pete's sake. They ate Buddhas for breakfast. Well, that was a weird image, she granted.

But even so, with Earl off her, Shelby thought of Hemana and how love was still in the air. She unzipped the tent door and a breeze of fresh ocean-swept air wafted in. The sky was a dazzling azure. In the distance, the waves in the ocean rumbled.

Earl flossed his teeth. He was concerned that the enamel covering one of his molars was wearing down. "One of my teeth feels sand-papery," he called to Shelby. "Could you come in here and feel it for me?"

"I am not sticking my hand in your mouth, Earl. Your tooth is fine. Now hurry up. I want to get down to the beach." Visions of Hemana's golden body danced in her mind's eye.

"I still have to brush," he said.

"Whatever." Also, Shelby wanted to see if what they'd experienced yesterday had actually happened. It was as if they'd parachuted into the cove toughened Navy SEAL warriors, but over the course of a few hours had turned into zoned-out drug-addicted Polynesian cult members. Earl was finally done.

OOPS-A-NAVY

She led him by the hand. "Earl, something tells me it's all happening at the beach. I do believe it. I do believe it's true."

"Well, that sounds like a song somehow, Shelby, but I think you're right." He ran his tongue over the sand-papery molar that was obsessing him. Yes, its surface was definitely scratchy. "You sure you can't check my tooth real quick?"

"Yes!"

As they walked, the rumble of the breakers grew louder. They turned a corner around a thicket, and the beach opened up before them. They stopped walking as if paralyzed by the beauty.

"Earl, are we still hallucinating?"

Earl realized he'd forgotten to use his anti-cavity rinse, but the scene really was stunning. "Probably. But if we are or aren't, it *is* pretty."

"Pretty just begins to describe it." The pinkish-orange sky at the horizon was turning an exquisite shimmering blue, rows of puffy white clouds rolling in. The rocks were lighter colored now, no longer the dark, ominous presence from last night, seemingly more rounded than jagged, and striped with tide rings. "This place is *so* different from where I grew up."

"It certainly ain't Kansas, Toto."

Shelby again seriously considered Bull's okay to terminate Earl if circumstances warranted. And if circumstances didn't quite warrant that extreme action, they certainly were getting close.

"Well, I can see we haven't scared you away." Hemana and a beautiful brunette, wearing a powder-blue T-shirt decorated with palm trees, walked up.

"Hemana." Shelby was breathless upon seeing him again. "Hi."

Earl quickly fixated on the brunette. She had luscious brown hair falling over her shoulders, a white orchid behind her ear and wore red lip-gloss. He said, "Well, hell-o."

The young woman smiled demurely.

Shelby felt so good and so in love with Hemana, it took great strength of mind to recall that they'd been drugged. And who was this brunette anyway? "Hemana, the mushroom smoothie? Was that a *magic* mushroom smoothie?"

Hemana smiled. Oh God, he was soooo sexy. "I don't know what kind of mushrooms they are, Shelby. All I know is that me, my father and my father's father have been enjoying them for hundreds of years."

"Well, they are good." Shelby smiled back. *Will you marry me?*

Earl crossed his arms over his chest to flaunt his biceps for the brunette. "And what is your name?"

"Talia."

Shelby was wondering about the pretty woman too. She turned to her. "And…uh…how do you and Hemana know each other?"

The woman smiled pleasantly. "He is my spirit brother."

"Spirit brother." Shelby nodded but wondered what the hell that meant. Although it wasn't a real Buddha-nature notion, she was thinking she might have to kill her.

"We're having another gathering at the beach tonight," Hemana said. "We hope the universe once more graces us with your awesome presence." He took Talia's hand, and they started walking away.

"Uh." Shelby wasn't happy seeing them touching. "What's a spirit brother?" she called.

But the couple continued on and disappeared into the woods.

Shelby turned to Earl. He suddenly looked *so* Earl. "Well, what do you think?"

Earl, still lusting over Talia, finally said, "About what?"

"About what's happening here, for Pete's sake! About the magic mushroom smoothie. The harmonic convergence. The Samoan hunk and brunette tramp."

OOPS-A-NAVY

Earl shrugged.

Shelby knew where he was coming from. A pleasant hallucinatory lethargy had descended upon her too. Hemana—she wanted to have his baby. She envisioned her life with him. After they would have steamy sex every morning, she would braid his hair. Then they would take Hemana Jr. down to the beach and teach him the ways of the benevolent surf god. Only no magic mushroom smoothie for Jr. until he was of age.

But no matter how pleasant Shelby's reverie, one thought simply wouldn't go away—they were Navy SEALs on a mission to find Senator Canfield and save the world from nuclear war! She grabbed Earl's bad arm.

"Ow!" He pulled away. "Why did you do that?"

"Because can't you see what's happening here? We're losing our connection with the mission."

"And what's so wrong with that? Shelby, I've been too uptight for too long. After all that crazy Hell Week training the Navy put us through, this island-living stuff is hitting the spot. And so is Talia, and she's hitting a very specific hot and stimulating spot."

Yeah, his fascination with Talia wasn't surprising. "Earl, you're just after everything with a skirt."

"She wore a bikini bottom."

"You know what I meant."

"And He-man?"

"Heman*a*. That's different."

"Oh?"

"Okay, so I got bowled over by the Samoan god. But I'm coming out of it. Earl, we can't forget our mission."

He shrugged again.

Shelby too could feel herself getting sucked back into the peaceful island vibe. And Hemana was everything she ever wanted. Who cared about missions or SEALs or nuclear war? But

81

still… "We need to get back to the tent."

"I thought we might look for seashells. With the tide being out, this is the best time of day for it."

"Earl." Shelby knew there was only one thing that could get them back on track.

"Shelby, why do we need to go back?"

She got in his face. "We need to check in with Bull Gompers."

* * *

They picked a couple of pineapples on their way back to the tent, hacking them open with machetes. Then Shelby set up her smart phone to call Bull Gompers. "Serious now," she warned Earl. She knew the poison-drug blow dart might be interacting with the magic mushroom smoothie further muddling his already muddled brain.

"Do you think Talia has a boyfriend?" he asked.

Of course it could just be the horniness thing. "Earl!" She entered the secret encryption key into her phone.

The call connected.

"Bull, can you hear me?" Shelby angled the phone's camera onto Earl. "Earl's here with me too."

The rear admiral's face flushed. "Did you just call me Bull?"

"No, no, Admiral." Shelby's heart pounded in her chest. Her mind raced. "I said 'cool,' because I was happy the connection went through."

"I could have sworn you said Bull."

"She did say Bull." Earl smiled idiotically.

"What was that?" Bull's face scrunched up.

"Hang on. Hang on." Shelby put the phone down and punched Earl on his bad arm. She picked up the phone. "Okay, I'm back, Admiral. I had to scare off a herd of wild boar that

OOPS-A-NAVY

rushed our camp. Now what were you saying?"

"Ryder." Bull's glasses were steaming and she removed them. "You better not be messing with me. I'll de-SEAL you both instantly."

Shelby was thinking, would that really be so bad? Hemana, the beach, mushroom smoothies. But she said, "No, Admiral. I've got things fully under control down here. A hundred percent."

"Well, you better." Bull's glasses cleared and she put them back on. "Okay, brief me."

Shelby's sea legs were back under her. Earl was still a liability of course, but at least she had the terminate order and wouldn't be putting up with much more of his nonsense before she implemented it. "Well, we landed safely in Candlebrake Cove."

"Well, I know that! But what about Senator Canfield? Have you located him?"

"Uh…"

"Ryder!"

"We think we have, Admiral."

"Several of him," Earl chipped in.

"What was that?" Bull's glasses steamed again.

"It's the wild boars, Admiral." Shelby glared at Earl. "They're a real nuisance down here, making strange grunts that sound like human voices."

"Where's Bernstein again?"

Shelby reluctantly focused the phone's camera on him.

Earl offered up a little wave. "Yo."

"How are you doing with the effects of the blow dart?" Bull waited.

"Honestly?"

Shelby turned the camera back onto herself. "Admiral, Bernstein is still not quite himself yet."

"Put him back on, Ryder."

Shelby had no choice. She aimed the camera at him.

Earl was coherent enough to realize he didn't want to jeopardize his situation. Not with beautiful Talia around. He bucked up. "Admiral, you know I would never give you anything but my utmost honest response. I am still experiencing slight effects of the blow dart poison drug, though no more than one might after visiting the dentist and receiving a substantial, but not fatal, overdose of nitrous oxide."

Shelby rolled her eyes and checked the screen. Bull looked confused. Shelby turned the camera back onto herself. "He's coming around, Admiral. He'll be himself in no time."

"He'd better be, Ryder." Bull slammed her fist down on a desk. "Now quit wasting my and the Navy's time and fill me in on Senator Canfield!"

Shelby bit the inside of her cheek. "Well, we firmly believe he may be in Candlebrake Cove. We've made great inroads with the locals, and some have even told us they've seen him in the woods."

"In the woods?"

"Yes. As you know the area is infested with Russian spies, but our contacts have discovered that several descendants of the legendary communist Che Guevara also live in the surrounding woods, and that Senator Canfield may have considered joining them."

"He considered becoming a commie?"

Shelby breathed in deep. "It looks that way, but I don't know if anything's that simple, Admiral. The senator may have been influenced by Che's relatives, yes, but Che's relatives have been influenced by the Russian spies. Word is the senator is open to the Guevarian influence but repelled by the Russian. It's not dissimilar to what's happening in the Middle East with the Sunni-Shia geopolitical push-pull."

"Ryder, that is the most disjointed bunch of hogwash I ever

heard. Look, just find the damn senator. Find him or you'll be back in Kansas watching the grass grow!"

The screen went blank.

* * *

The day passed rapidly. Yes, Shelby and Earl were SEALs. Yes, they were feeling guilty about enjoying the magic mushroom smoothies and lazy pleasures of island living. But they figured this was just a phase they were going through. They'd snap out of it and do the right thing—they'd get Senator Canfield back. And okay, there was the threat of nuclear war thing, but besides that, there was no gigantic hurry.

Since this could be their last day there, at dusk they happily took their places at the gathering ceremony on the beach. With relatively non-drug-addled minds, they could see that the people sitting around the fire were actually pretty normal. Oh, some were dressed nicer than others (one woman in a scarlet silk dress sat on a little stool and wore an impressive string of pearls), but almost everybody else was in shorts and T-shirts. Hemana was running the show again, and both Shelby and Earl were glad that he and Talia were not sitting next to each other.

The moment of truth came quickly and the magic-mushroom-smoothie chalice came around. This time the SEALs took big gulps. Hey, it could be their last day there!

Whoa! Shelby thought. It didn't take long for the sound of Hemana's voice to change, and the fire was changing colors again too, as were the hard and fast edges of the people gathered, outlines blurring and merging into one another. Shelby felt she was becoming all mind and no body. A universal mind. Hemana raised a hand, and Shelby thought his arm was a fiery sword and she screamed. But no one seemed to hear, or if they did, they weren't troubled by it. And actually, maybe she hadn't screamed

—she couldn't be sure.

Hemana waxed eloquently about love and consciousness again. About how love was taking over the world. Then he started rambling about how they were all spirit protectors. Or did he say spirit animals? Or did he say anything at all? But he must've said something like that because people started giving testimonies. This one was a wolf. That one a frog. Another a rabbit. They went around the circle.

Just before it was Shelby's turn, she looked and saw that *everyone* sitting in the circle was Senator Canfield! What! Then just as quickly, they were back and he was gone.

"Shelby?" Hemana smiled. "Would you like to share with the group?"

The hallucinating SEAL stood. She was slightly reassured that Hemana was back and that he and the others weren't all Senator Canfields. For certainly, that would've presented a problem if they had to find all the Senator Canfields. Issues would arise. Which Senator Canfield to believe? That sort of thing.

"Shelby?"

"Oh, right." She wiped her sweaty hands on her shorts. "I… am…an otter." An otter? she thought. But no, something deep within her felt as if she was. Not that it was a dream or a hallucination. She was an otter. Slipping in and out of the water, building dams, catching fish. She had the wisdom of the earth, of the wild, within her. It was absolutely amazing. Earl was next.

He didn't hesitate. "I am a hawk and my mission in life is to swoop in and carry Talia away in my talons." Hmm, he thought. "Talia in my talons"—nicely alliterative. He could work that into a love poem he'd write her.

Shelby couldn't say exactly how it happened, but Hemana had been going on about the beauty of nature and how man's repression had destroyed its original purity. How in the beginning, people had no shame and considered their naked bodies beautiful.

OOPS-A-NAVY

Next thing Shelby knew, they were all skinny-dipping in the cove.

Shelby, still feeling like an otter, had no fear of the water. And at least it was relatively dark out. She was afraid to look at Hemana though, and she didn't want to look at Earl or have him see her.

He was following, practically shadowing, Talia into the water so closely it was creeping Shelby out. "Earl."

He turned to her. She saw his nakedness and looked away, but she asked, "Are we really doing this?"

"I think so, Shelby," he said. "I mean, it feels like we are."

"So, do you really think you're a hawk?"

He sighed. "Uh, yeah, I'm pretty sure I am. How about you? Are you still an otter?"

"I think so. But I mean, whether we think we're these things or not, isn't it odd that we're skinny-dipping with strangers?"

"I don't know. To tell you the truth, I don't consider Talia a stranger anymore. I think she's, like Hemana was saying, my spirit sister. But I gotta admit it's weird being naked with you. And I can see you've put most of that extra weight on in your thighs."

That snapped Shelby out of her trance. "Why, you're no hawk, Earl. You're nothing but a dog!" She pushed him hard and he plopped into the water, making a belly-flop sound. She headed back to the beach.

"Sister Shelby," Hemana called to her as she approached, his luminous eyes seemingly glowing in his head. He was still at the campfire with everyone else, including Earl, and they were all dry and fully clothed.

Chapter Eleven

In the morning, Shelby woke to find her and Earl sleeping on a pile of palm tree fronds in a cabana where the cove met the sea. The waves splashed onto the rocks with more power here, blasts of the salty water shooting up. Shelby shook Earl awake.

"Earl, what the heck happened last night?"

Earl rubbed the sleep from his eyes. "I saw Elvis again."

"And I saw multiple Senator Canfields."

"Wow. Must've been a different batch of mushrooms than the first night."

"Did you feel like we were skinny-dipping?"

He shook his head. "But for a stretch there Elvis and I were shucking sugar cane in a field."

"Really?"

"Yeah, and it was hard work. I didn't like it at all."

"Are you still a hawk?"

He sat up and rubbed his bad arm. "Uh, okay, I remember that now. Yeah, I guess I am."

"Earl, I don't know how to say this, but I think we've become members of a cult."

His hands gripped the palm tree fronds. "Don't say that."

"Why not?"

"Because I want to marry Talia, and my parents would freak if they knew she was in a cult."

"Oh boy."

"Do you think she's Jewish?"

Shelby shook her head. "That's unlikely."

"Damn!"

The sound of the waves bashing the rocks was so loud they didn't hear a couple approaching on the beach.

OOPS-A-NAVY

"Earl, Shelby!" Ashley Harrington called.

The Harringtons stood outside the cabana. Earl was suddenly very confused. Like that song "Torn Between Two Lovers." Not that he was lovers with either Ashley or Talia, but that was his first thought. He reprimanded himself for being too dependent on popular culture. He was a poet, for Pete's sake. He ought to have a more sophisticated sensibility. "Shelby, it's the Harringtons."

Shelby turned and first off was surprised it was getting dark already—they must've slept through the whole day. And yeah, now the next surprise—the Harringtons. Thinking back to when they'd all been at the Diamond Cubano Restaurante, Shelby certainly wasn't happy about the way Ashley had run off with Earl. And that coupled with Manuel's insistence that Ashley was a spy, Shelby wasn't trusting her, or Preston, for that matter.

"Ashley, Preston," she said. "What are you doing in Candlebrake Cove?"

Ashley laughed. "Simple, Shelby. Word filtered down at De La Rata Golf Course that Senator Canfield might be here. The country club grapevine is powerful."

"So you came all the way out here just to find him?"

"Shelby, you have no idea how much we miss having him in our golfing foursome."

Okay, Ashley seemed sincere. Shelby's resistance to her was breaking down. "All right, I hear you." She gave the dentist a hug.

Next up, Earl presented himself for a hug as well. Ashley pulled down the zipper of her beach jacket, showing not a little cleavage. "There's my big boy."

They hugged, Earl even kissing the stacked woman on the cheek, while Shelby looked at Preston, who was lackadaisically checking his Rolex. What was up with that?

* * *

As Shelby and Earl stood talking to the Harringtons, Shelby had a flashback to the day before. The Senator Canfield clones. The imagined, or real, skinny-dipping. (The imagined, or real, comment by Earl about her chunky thighs.) And she was still feeling like an otter. Even feeling that she had otter buck teeth. She couldn't wait to get to a mirror. But even more important was figuring out what the heck was going on. *Were* they in a cult? Was Senator Canfield there? Were several of him? Was Hemana the man of her dreams? Was getting together with him practical? (She couldn't see his love of going bare-chested working in Kansas.) But first and foremost was dealing with the Harringtons. How odd that they just showed up.

Shelby tried to pick their brains again, hopefully tactfully. "So again, forgive me, Ashley and Preston, we did a little partying last night—"

"We drank magic mushroom smoothies and got whacked out of our minds." Earl hummed the melody from "Torn Between Two Lovers."

Shelby raised an eyebrow at Earl. It was a warning look that used to work. Who knew if it would now?

Ashley said, "Oh, Preston and I love a good magic 'shroom now and then too. They're so fun. But I've never had them in smoothies. How clever!"

Shelby twirled her hair. Hmm. That was a surprise—so the Harringtons were druggies. Probably addicted to opioids too. But gosh, this otter obsession and the accompanying fear of big front teeth still troubled her mightily. (She wasn't that vain, but she might want to have a family someday, especially since it looked like neither her artist brother nor her sister, who worked at Bob's Mega Burger, would ever have kids.) And this Ashley was a dentist. "Ashley, do you think you could take a quick look at my teeth? Like as a professional courtesy, where you don't charge me?"

OOPS-A-NAVY

"Why, sure."

"I'd appreciate it."

Earl piped up, "She thinks she's an otter."

Ashley laughed. "Oh, Earl."

Shelby forced a smile. "Just check 'em please. But it's got to be for free. My dentist back home is this Ukrainian who rips me off constantly—but he does good work and I like his hygienist."

"Yeah, yeah, free, Shelby, no worries." Ashley turned to Preston. "Let me have a pair of exam gloves."

He snapped out a couple of blue latex gloves from a fanny pack. "Here you go."

Ashley gloved up and turned back to Shelby. "Now open wide."

Shelby blushed. This felt silly as it was the first time she'd ever had an otter big front teeth obsession. "It's just the front ones. They just feel...they just feel...*big*."

Ashley did a double-take. "Big?"

"I know it sounds weird, but I've been feeling as if I look like Alvin the chipmunk lately."

"I've heard weirder," Ashley said unconvincingly. She turned to Preston. "Preston, a tape measure?"

Preston dug into the fanny pack and produced a Stanley stainless-steel tape measure with an auto-locking feature. "Here you go."

Ashley pulled out the tape a foot or so and let it snap back. "All right, sweetie. Again, open."

The dentist measured Shelby's front teeth. "No, they're absolutely normal size. They fit within the parameters of healthy adult female teeth."

"Wow, that's a relief." Shelby was opening up more and more to Ashley. She seemed so kind, and she liked magic mushrooms. Earl, on the other hand, she was going to throttle. His only excuse again would be the interaction between the mushroom smoothie and the poison-drug blow dart. It was Preston alone she still didn't get. He was a mystery. She especially wondered why he didn't mind his wife being slutty with Earl.

"Yep, girl." Ashley nodded. "Those pearly whites of yours are as normal as normal can be."

"So, Preston?" Shelby, relieved, put her hands in her pockets. "What do you do?"

"Me?"

"Ha ha, silly," Ashley said. "Are there any other Prestons here?"

"Oh, right." Preston dabbed his forehead with a white silk handkerchief. "I'm the CEO of Blackstone Alpha Dynamics. Well, BAD for short."

"Oh," Shelby said. "Thanks." But she wasn't entirely satisfied with that answer. "And what does BAD do?"

"Well." Preston suppressed an impish smile. "BAD does good."

"Oh, Preston." Ashley mussed his hair. "*You're* b-a-d!"

But Shelby still wasn't satisfied. "What kind of good?"

"Okay, we're an international arms dealer with a seventy-five percent market share worldwide. We produce warships, aircraft carriers and are the world's largest supplier of nuclear submarines."

Shelby *was* satisfied with that answer, but still, if Preston supplied all that stuff to the Navy, did he know Bull Gompers? It sent a shiver down her spine.

"Well, Shelby and Earl." Ashley again. "It's been great catching up, but Preston and I are plum tuckered out from traveling all day and need to head into town to get a hotel room so we can catch some sleep."

"I've got an idea." Earl brightened. "Shelby and I are staying in an inflated tent that will easily sleep four. Why don't you bunk with us?"

OOPS-A-NAVY

Oh God, Shelby thought. It was almost too much to think about. Everything whirling through her mind. Hemana. Bull Gompers. Cults. Mushroom smoothies (she was convinced Earl, anyway, should be cut off). Multiple Senator Canfields. And now she was expected to host company at the tent?! She thought of how she'd left it. The place was a mess, and she needed to find a stream to do laundry. But the Harringtons were never going to find a hotel in town because there was no town, and Ashley had been nice enough to measure her teeth *and* it was getting late. How could she say no? "Why, that's right, Earl," she said, smiling while thinking, *You numbskull.* "There's plenty of room."

*   *   *

"I'll just run ahead to check if everything is okay." Shelby hurried off. She was going to brain Earl. The aggravation he was causing her was getting unbearable, which reminded her of Bull's termination option. The thought gave her comfort.

At the tent, she took a palm frond and swept out the crumbs from the French bread they'd eaten with spaghetti. She noticed Earl had spilled marinara sauce on the floor, so she wiped it with a pre-moistened commercial towelette (which they were running low on—Earl was a mess to clean up after). And speaking of Earl, Shelby was tired of his two-faced approaches to women. First, Ashley was his all-in-all. Then Talia was. But now that Ashley's back, he's forgotten about Talia. Typical man. "Phew!" She looked around the tent. The hurry-up cleaning would have to do. She could hear the others talking outside.

Ashley poked her head in. "Oh, how quaint!"

"Thanks, Ashley." Shelby was liking her more and more.

The four of them settled in the tent. A battery-powered lantern on the floor cast strange, shifting shadows. Shelby thought it may have been because they were moving, or it could have been the aftereffects from the mushroom smoothie playing with her mind. And look at that. Earl scooted right next to Ashley. Shelby drilled him with a look. "I wonder what Talia would say if she saw you now?"

Ashley turned to Earl. "Who's Talia?"

He ran his hands through his hair. "Ah, just this island girl. She means nothing to me."

Ashley moved away from him. "She means nothing, eh?"

"Okay." Earl slumped forward. "I wanted to marry her because she was so young and beautiful, but in hindsight, I really think it was the effects of the poison-drug blow dart talking."

Ashley tilted her head, studied him, and then her voice softened. "You were hit with a poison-drug blow dart?"

He nodded.

"Well, why didn't you tell me?" She moved back to him and put her arm around him.

Shelby looked at Preston. He seemed bored. She was wondering what kind of sick, twisted open marriage he and Ashley had.

Earl pushed his thigh into Ashley's. "I meant to, but I was distracted by the pain."

"It really hurt, huh?"

Earl smiled masculinely. "Navy SEALs are trained to endure pain."

"Oh my gosh, you said that you were Navy SEALs before, but I thought you were joking. You're really a Navy SEAL!" Her mouth fell open and she stared at him wide-eyed. She turned to Preston. "Preston, they're Navy SEALs! They probably know Bull Gompers!"

Shelby jumped in at this point. Earl, again, was blowing their cover. "No, we're not Navy SEALs. A seal is just his spirit animal. At least that's the way it seemed to him when he was all jacked up on the mushroom smoothie."

OOPS-A-NAVY

"You're wrong, Shelby." Earl leaned against the tent wall. "My spirit animal is a hawk."

"You were a seal-hawk, Earl." Shelby was panting. If she'd had one handy, she would've hit him with another poison-drug blow dart.

Shelby could see by the look on Ashley's face she wasn't buying it. This whole thing was turning into a first-class mess. What if the Harringtons called Bull Gompers? It could get them pulled off the mission. Hell, it could get them de-SEALed. Shelby's heart fluttered and filled with suspicion. Who really were these Harringtons anyway? Just a quirky couple with an open marriage? Or spies tracking not Senator Canfield, but her and Earl! She turned to Preston. "All right, Preston, I need you to stand."

"What?"

"You heard me. Up you go." Shelby wasn't fooling.

The arms dealer stood. "Okay. Now what?"

"Now this." She patted him down. She found a cell phone in one pocket and a switchblade in another. "And what about this, eh?" She held the knife up to his face.

"It's for protection." Preston hardly seemed flustered. "I'm sure you've heard there are cannibals on the island."

What? Really? No, she hadn't. Could Bull Gompers have purposefully misled her about that because she knew cannibals creeped her out? "You sure about that?"

"Trust me, I've had personal experience with them." Preston took off his blazer and rolled up his sleeve. His forearm was brutally scarred. "They started gnawing on my arm, and fortunately a SWAT team arrived just before they could consume me entirely."

"Gross." Shelby wiped the sweat from her brow. Cannibals. Yikes! "But even so, you could've punctured the tent with the switchblade and then where would we be?"

"Well." Preston's face soured. "It wasn't open."

Shelby looked at his arm again and cringed. "Do me a favor and pull your sleeve down, will you? I'm on the verge of throwing up looking at that." She made eye contact with Ashley and nodded. "Okay, now you, Toots."

Ashley turned to Earl. "Are you going to let her call me that? It sounds sexist."

"I don't know." Earl paged through one of his notebooks. "It doesn't sound so bad to me. People are just too sensitive these days."

"Earl!" Ashley cried.

"Up." Shelby was waiting.

The dentist stood. "Why, I never…"

Shelby patted her down and found—nothing. "That's odd." She turned to Earl. "Okay, hand me her purse."

"No!" Ashley moved to grab the purse, but Earl whisked it behind his back, and gave it to Shelby.

"All right, Ashley, you can sit down." Shelby held up the brightly colored piñata-like purse that must've weighed twenty pounds. "Let's see, what do we have here?" She pulled out a mirror. She flashed a wicked look at Ashley. "What's this?!"

"A mirror."

"Well, I know it's a mirror, Toots, but why do you have it? Who were you signaling?"

"Oh my God." Ashley massaged her temples.

"And this?" Shelby held up a canister of pepper spray. "Planning on using it on me?"

Ashley leaned on Earl. "If I got the chance."

"Really?" Shelby flicked the switchblade open.

"I was joking," Ashley said. "Shelby, what's gotten into you? And have you forgotten I gave you a free dental exam?"

Shelby nodded. "Well, that's true, but I'm just not sure about you guys anymore, and I think the mushroom smoothie is making me paranoid. I am from Kansas, after all."

Ashley took a quick breath. "Yeah, that's understandable—it can't be easy being from Kansas."

Shelby went back to searching the purse. "And this?" She held up a brown-hued prescription bottle, and in the process dropped the switchblade. "Oh, look what you made me do!"

Ashley scowled. "I didn't make you!"

Shelby dropped to her knees and extricated the switchblade. The weight of having four people in the tent made the air scream through the tear the knife made, like the sound of a tea kettle boiling. "Earl, did you pack duct tape in the emergency kit?"

"I thought you did."

"Earl, don't you care…" Shelby brandished the switchblade at him. "…if the tent is deflated?"

"Not really, Shelby." He put his arm around Ashley. "I could go for some more of that mushroom smoothie, though."

Oh my God! Shelby thought. He's addicted! But honestly, a mushroom smoothie didn't sound like a bad idea at this point. She really needed something to calm her nerves. "Well, where could we get some this time of night? It's hardly like there's a convenience store around."

"Couldn't you ask that Hemana guy?" Earl figured that was their best shot.

"Well, I could if I could find him." Shelby rose, grabbed a flashlight and headed out into the pitch-black night to look for the Samoan stud.

* * *

It was all so much to think about, Shelby mused as she shined the flashlight on the dirt path. Yeah, maybe a few swallows of the magic mushroom smoothie would be just what they all needed, and then tomorrow she could get back to fulfilling her mission as a SEAL, find the senator and save the world from nuclear war. But Earl, Earl was going to be trouble. He was turning into a real islander and seemed to have crossed the point of no return—she might have to terminate him. Which would be a relief actually. She was looking forward to it.

She'd heard Hemana lived in the highlands above the cove, so she made her way up there. Getting the mushroom smoothies was a boring assignment, akin to a hallucinogenic beer run. Still, it was hardly a lot of fun walking alone in the dark, especially with that talk earlier of cannibals. But she could hear the rumble of the waves, and the sea breeze picked up, comforting her.

Finally, high up in the mountains she came across a makeshift mailbox fashioned out of coconuts and seashells, with Hemana's name on it in purple magic marker. So this must be his hut, or actually huts because there were two of them. The huts were on a sandy mound, topped with thatched roofs and were surrounded by tall palm trees, some of which had not a few fronds hanging down as if they'd been damaged in a hurricane. A creek ran in front of the huts, the clear water gurgling gently, flowing toward the cove.

As Shelby walked up to the first hut, she pointed the flashlight at the entrance of the other hut. Two Komodo dragons sat there like sentries, the giant lizards spitting their long deadly tongues out like cobras. Hmm. Shelby knocked on the sheet metal door decorated with a peace sign.

The beautiful island girl Talia answered. She wore a white halter-top and a paisley wrap-around. It was pathetic—the woman was so pretty and the picture of island calm. But Shelby didn't want to jump to conclusions because at this point she didn't know that Hemana and Talia were anything more than the spirit brother and sister as Hemana had claimed. "Is Hemana around?"

"Wait here." The beauty walked off.

Shelby was gratified that the inside of the hut was nothing

special. Just some gear stowed in the corner: coolers and ropes, as well as towels and bathing suits hung on the rafters to dry.

Here came Hemana. He wore white jeans, a scarlet silk shirt and a puka shell necklace. "Blessed friend, welcome to my humble abode."

Shelby cocked her head to the side. She hadn't been going to say anything, but she couldn't help herself. "Talia—does she live with you?"

He brushed his fingers through his beautiful black hair. He smiled and just kept gazing at Shelby, who could feel herself melting in his presence. "Can I offer you a seat?" He gestured to a mattress next to an oscillating fan. "It's not much but it's comfortable."

She sat. He wasn't answering her question, but he was so handsome she decided to let him slide. "Thank you."

"Blessings to you from the eternal one of the ages." He smiled again. Such perfect white teeth. Shelby wondered if he'd had them bleached. "Would you like to offer a small libation of gratitude to the gods with me?"

That's what Shelby was there for. But she was there to get libations for the others too. But simply being in Hemana's dazzling presence was enough to make her forget about that. It was enough to make her forget about everything. She shrugged her approval.

Hemana clapped his hands in a particular sequence.

Talia appeared with two plastic cups. She handed one cup to Hemana, the other to Shelby.

Seeing Talia again, Shelby's jealousy surged. What, was Talia a servant? A sex slave? His wife? Shelby looked at Hemana and said, "Bottom's up," and drank down the libation. She figured she'd ask before she was too impaired, "And can I get some of this to go? I've got people visiting that also like to offer libations."

Again, Hemana clapped his hands, this time a different sequence, triggering Talia's disappearance into the hut before returning with a gallon of mushroom smoothie. Shelby thanked Talia, who already was seeming liquidy as she disappeared into the hut again. And now Shelby was sitting across from the Dalai Lama. At least she thought it was the Dalai Lama, but even so, he spoke in Hemana's voice. But what Hemana was saying she would never know. It was distorted, like audio hieroglyphics. Funny, though, she wondered about the Komodo dragons outside the other hut and just as she did, she was suddenly walking by them to the door of that hut.

Shelby told herself she really should just leave, but the lure of what was inside the second hut drove her on. She pushed the door open. The interior was not unlike Hemana's hut but it was barer. Barer and it had a bright turquoise-colored metal door on the far side of it. A hemp chain dangled from the ceiling, supporting a miniature hut from which a stick of incense burned. But Shelby couldn't smell the incense. Odd, she thought.

"Quite a difference from my hut, isn't it?" Hemana appeared at her side. This was crazy. How did he get there? Was he solid? She touched his bicep. Yep. It was real all right—and felt good!

"So what's behind the door?" Shelby thought the door seemed Mexican somehow, the turquoise coloring maybe. A rusty lock hung on it. It was so different from everything else she'd seen on the island. That's if she was truly seeing it because in the blink of an eye, she was back outside—shining the flashlight on the dirt path, an occasional insect flitting in and out of the light's spray—holding the gallon of mushroom smoothie under her arm, on her way back to the tent.

* * *

In an instant, Shelby was at the tent. It was as if she'd

hyperspaced there. The tent was deflated now, a shell of its former self. Inside, Earl, Preston and Ashley sat around glumly. Shelby shook her head. "All right, besides the tent deflating…" She felt like vegging out, but her Navy SEAL discipline didn't allow her to go there. Not yet anyway. "…why all the cat-that-ate-the-canary faces?"

Preston sat on one side of the tent, Ashley and Earl on the other, lipstick all over Earl's cheeks and collar.

Preston spoke first saying, "These things happen."

"What things?"

Ashley sighed.

"Earl?" Shelby was losing patience.

He shrugged.

She kept staring at them. Slowly, they were becoming less solid, porous. The mushroom smoothie was messing with her mind. She had to act fast before they turned into alien-life forms. "What the hell, you're all looking like you just called Bull Gompers."

Earl. Finally. "We didn't call her."

"So then why all the sad faces? I'm not sad. Come on." She held up the jug of mushroom smoothie.

Preston announced, "She called us."

"What?!" Even hallucinating Shelby was wary of Bull Gompers. "How?"

Preston crossed his arms. "On the emergency radio band."

Oh God, Shelby thought. She did her best to be brave. "So she called. Earl, you covered for me?"

Earl nodded. "But she more than called."

Shelby felt her heart drop into her stomach.

Earl frowned. "She's coming."

Bull Gompers coming to Candlebrake Cove sobered Shelby instantly. Earl was already cut off from more mushroom smoothie, and now the Harringtons weren't getting any either.

Bull's arrival was going to upset the apple cart big-time, and they said she was coming at zero nine hundred hours in the morning. Shelby wouldn't be any good to anyone in the mental shape she was in, so she took a few belts of the mushroom smoothie and lay down hoping sleep would rejuvenate her.

Chapter Twelve

The wind blew in hard from the east in the morning. Shelby hoped it wasn't La Nina, the Cuban climate cycle that could lead to the formation of a hurricane. But she didn't have time to think about the weather, so she shooed the Harringtons and Earl to the beach and chewed a huge wad of bubble gum, using it to seal the tear in the tent. Then she popped the emergency CO_2 cartridge to inflate the tent. She tidied things up to be white-glove clean so as to pass Bull Gomper's inevitable inspection. Now she too headed to the beach as zero nine hundred hours was only minutes away, and if Bull Gompers was anything, she was punctual.

It was sunny. No sign of a hurricane or tsunami, but even so, the trade winds were ripping, and the surf beyond the cove raised thunderous whitecaps. Earl was sitting with his arm around Ashley on the beach, Preston wandering along the shore looking for seashells. Shelby walked up. "I wouldn't be sitting with her like that if I were you, Earl."

"Yeah." Earl stood and looked down at Ashley. "Sorry, but Bull might get the wrong idea."

"I understand, Earl. From what Preston tells me, Bull has one heck of a powerful personality." Ashley stood too, then brushed the sand from Earl's butt.

"Quit touching him!" It shouldn't be bothering Shelby but it was.

"Look!" Preston pointed. "Up in the sky!"

Sure enough, a Navy helicopter emerged from behind the mountains, inspiring in Shelby a resurgence of patriotism and pride in being a SEAL! Earl, however, stuck on Ashley again, was still feeling substantially islander-ish. But if anybody could inspire the fear of God in a person it was Bull Gompers. An object, like a rock or a gnat or a FedEx package, fell from the helicopter. Oh boy, Shelby thought. She wished the wind wasn't blowing so hard, because Bull was getting shot across the sky like a spitball blown by a giant kid with tremendous lung capacity.

Preston, a grave seriousness in his eyes, said, "I hope they calculated her trajectory with the wind velocity, otherwise she's going to end up in Miami."

Seeing Bull falling from the sky like that, an eighty-five-year-old patriot, a hero, cleared the cobwebs of Shelby's 'shroom hangover. And Shelby had had it with Preston. He was so milquetoast, especially for an arms dealer. "Tell me, Preston, don't you care that your wife is being a slut with Earl? What kind of husband are you?"

Bull's chute opened, the familiar yellow and white with SEAL stamped on it in navy blue. Her tiny body being buffeted and rocked by the wind gusts.

Preston's brow furrowed. "Oh, my gosh, Shelby, I'm sorry. Yes, you're right, Ashley is a slut, but she isn't my wife. She's my sister."

Shelby almost fainted. How could she have been so dumb! They were brother and sister! It all made sense now. But Bull was getting blown toward the rock outcroppings. "Oh, Preston, I'm so sorry I accused you. Can I give you a hug?"

They hugged, but Bull was in trouble.

Earl was getting animated. Was he coming back to himself? "Looks like Bull will get impaled on the rock outcroppings!"

"All right." Shelby took charge. "Let's run and see where she lands."

"Good idea." Ashley was game too. "Come on, Preston."

Although it wasn't easy running in the sand, the group took off down the shore, but before they even reached the first rock outcropping, Bull had already drifted out of their line of sight.

"She's probably dead," Preston ventured, already sucking air.

OOPS-A-NAVY

"But I say we keep going. Hopefully we can find her body and bury it before the cannibals eat her."

Again, Shelby was rocked by hearing about cannibals. She was a woman of few fears but being eaten alive was definitely one of them. "We'll get her before they do, Preston."

"I hope so, because finding her half-eaten body would be so unpleasant."

"Yeah, right. But in the meantime, stop talking about it, will you?"

"You got it, Shelby."

Up the rock outcropping they went. Shelby couldn't help but think she saw evidence that cannibals had been there. Torn clothing abandoned. Sun-bleached femurs and sternums, rib cages, a few skulls. But she couldn't be sure—maybe the hallucinogenic effects of the mushroom smoothie were kicking in again. And certainly her concern for Bull was clouding her judgment. They were all breathing hard. The Harringtons, not trained to the same level of fitness as the SEALs, fell back. "Come on, Earl," Shelby encouraged. "We owe it to Bull to find her."

"I agree, Shelby." Earl was sweating profusely. Maybe sweating out the poison-drug blow dart effect? "But really, at her age, she should think about giving up parachuting."

That was a good point, Shelby thought, but now wasn't the time to consider it. "We'll talk about that later. Come on. She can't be that much farther."

Earl shielded his eyes from the sun and peered. "There's her chute. She's at the top of the mountain."

Shelby realized Earl was right—and not only was Bull at the top of the mountain she was also atop one of the palm trees surrounding Hemana's huts. "Oh boy. Earl, did you think to bring the tree-climbing cleats?"

"I did."

"Great!" Encouraged, Shelby thought things were starting to go their way. She looked up again and Bull's tiny octogenarian legs dangled like a turtle's, well, like a turtle that's been turned upside down anyway. "Bull!" she yelled. "We're coming!" That's when she heard hissing. "Uh-oh."

It was the Komodo dragons that had been outside Hemana's second hut. And they were heading straight for them! "Earl, you keep them engaged, and I'll outflank them and go help Bull. Give me the cleats."

Earl caught his breath. He felt he really had lost a lot of his conditioning. But what the hell was Shelby talking about? "Engage what, Shelby?"

She looked again and the Komodo dragons were gone. "Oh, for God's sake. Well, give me the cleats, and you stand at the base of the tree in case I fall."

"But you'll crush me. Remember all the weight you've put on."

"Earl!"

"All right."

At the palm tree, Bull was yelling, "Hurry. There are bugs in these palm fronds. They're crawling all over me."

Shelby hesitated before calling, "What kind of bugs?"

"Giant cockroaches!"

Shelby turned to Earl. "You really should be the one to get her."

"I don't like cockroaches either, Shelby. And the poison-drug blow dart has weakened my strength. I might not be able to get all the way to the top."

"Thanks a lot, Earl." Shelby sighed, looped the leather strap around the tree and dug her cleats into its spongy surface.

"Hurry!" Bull yelled. "They're in my hair. I think one's crawled into my bra."

"Just relax, Bull. Being upset isn't helping anything." Shelby was halfway up when she felt things hitting her like substantial snowflakes except they weren't cold or wet. It took a while to realize that the 'snowflakes' were actually giant cockroaches being shaken loose by Bull's agitation. "Stop moving, Bull!"

Earl, at the base of the tree, wasn't happy. "It's raining cockroaches down here! If you don't hurry, I'm leaving."

"Hear that, Bull?" A cockroach landed in Shelby's hair. "Ah!" Her hands were holding the strap. She couldn't let go. The giant bug crawled along her cheek, then across her lips. Finally, Shelby spat and the bug went flying.

"Hey!" Earl cried. "I just got hit with a hocker!"

Shelby laughed, happy she'd hit Earl with the hocker, but she had to focus on Bull now. She grabbed Bull's tiny quivering legs. "I've got you now, Bull. Stop squirming."

Bull kicked and caught Shelby in the breast.

"Hey, what the hell, Bull?!"

"You call me Bull again, Ryder, and I'll have you de-SEALed before you can say—"

"Cockroach?" Shelby let go of Bull's legs and moved a notch down the tree.

"Hey." Bull went back to dangling. "Where did you go?"

Shelby sighed. "I'm not so sure I want to save someone who kicks me in the breast."

"Did I get you in the breast?" Bull sounded remorseful. "If I did I'm sorry. I was trying to kick you in the head."

Shelby moved another notch down the tree. "Like that's supposed to make me feel better?"

"Well, I can't have you calling me Bull. I'm a rear admiral for God's sake."

"You know what?" Shelby looked down at Earl, who was joined by the Harringtons. (She was still processing that they were brother and sister. Who knew?) "While I've been here in Candlebrake Cove, I've learned a lot about universal peace and love radiating out into the world's consciousness, and those are lessons I never learned in Navy SEAL Hell Week. I think those are lessons you might do well to learn yourself."

"Well…" Bull seemed to be thinking. "There's something to what you're saying, Ryder, but remember I'm older and it's harder for me to change. How about this? You don't call me Bull and I won't kick you again? Deal?"

Earl yelled, "What the hell are you two doing up there?"

"I tell you what." Shelby felt like she was getting somewhere with her. "Throw in radiating a little love out into the universe, and yeah, I'll call it a deal."

Bull raised her eyebrows. She pursed her lips. She took a deep breath, hocked her throat and spat but the trade winds caught it.

"Hey!" Earl cried again. "I just got hit by another hocker!"

Shelby was coming back to herself, Bull's presence returning a healthy dose of clear-headedness. Earl seemed to be more himself too. The Harringtons were brother and sister. It was all good. "So what do you say, *Admiral*?"

Bull nodded. "All right, Ryder. You got a deal. Now get me down."

* * *

Shelby helped Bull down from the palm tree. They let her lay at the base of the tree to rest before heading down to the beach. Earl and Preston then offered to carry her, but she insisted on walking. She was happy to see Preston again (secretly she was angling for a sweet position lobbying at his arms firm when she retired) and meet his sister. But besides that, she was all business, even to the point of telling Preston and Ashley to drop back because she had to talk about classified information with Shelby and Earl.

"Okay," Bull said. She climbed down a rock. They were

OOPS-A-NAVY

almost to the beach. "Brief me on the situation here. In your earlier communication, you said locals reported seeing Senator Canfield in the woods?"

"Yes, but it's been confusing, Admiral." Shelby didn't want to lie, but how could she tell her the truth? Hallucinogenic mushroom smoothies. Multiple Senator Canfields. Multiple Elvises, or was it Elvi? Bull just wouldn't understand. No, Shelby had to tell her something she could grasp. "It seems there's a propaganda campaign the Russians are pushing here. Strange things have been happening."

Bull took off her combat boots when they got to the beach. "Oh, the sand feels good on my bare feet. So nice and warm."

"Yes, it's warm." Shelby could feel a little bit of love radiating from Bull already. She was a woman of her word.

"Anyway, Ryder, back to Senator Canfield. You said he considered joining descendants of Che Guevara?"

Shelby rolled her eyes. She could hardly believe she'd told her that. But then again, it was more plausible than multiple Senator Canfields. "Yes."

"Well, that makes the most sense to me." Bull picked up a conch shell and put it to her ear. "The Russians influenced the Cubans—well, actually Che Guevara was Argentine, but they all speak the same damn language—and Canfield was seduced by their left-wing ideology. I mean, let's face it, Canfield is as close to being a commie as a US senator can get, being for free healthcare, college and tickets to NFL games. Yeah, I wouldn't be surprised if they made him the new Castro down here."

Hemana and Talia walked along the beach toward them.

"Admiral." Shelby was very careful with the name thing now. "Here come a couple of islanders we've cultivated. Actually, we've some concerns that they may be cult members, but we have received credible intel from them too. I'll introduce you."

Bull stared at Hemana like a teenager with a crush, then

turned to Shelby. A moment of near-tenderness. She adjusted her little Navy hat with the trident emblem on it. "Do I look okay?"

It was clear to Shelby that Bull was wowed by Hemana too. "You look fab, Admiral."

Bull smiled.

Shelby introduced Bull and thought she'd never seen the rear admiral more animated. She told jokes and talked about how she'd been a lifeguard at a beach just like this. The animation made her look thirty years younger. And Shelby watched Earl watching Talia and Ashley watching Earl watching Talia. Trouble was brewing. Lastly, Shelby watched Hemana and how he was with Talia. Yes, the guy was a dream. But Shelby was beginning to think that maybe the whole Candlebrake Cove experience was a dream too. Like the hut next to Hemana's with the turquoise-colored door and rusty lock on it. And the cannibal bones and Komodo dragons.

It seemed Bull had been calling her. "Yes, Admiral?"

"Wow, you were really lost in thought there, Ryder."

Tell me about it, Shelby thought. Hemana and Talia were down the beach now.

Bull smiled. "So that nice young man invited us to some sort of beach party tonight—"

"It's a cosmic ceremony," Earl explained.

"Whatever, Bernstein." The rear admiral kicked playfully at a wave that rushed up the golden sand. She turned back to Shelby. "I said we would be attending."

Shelby crossed her arms over her chest. "I don't know if that's a good idea, Admiral. As I was saying, although we consider them valuable contacts, we have concrete reasons to suspect their group is a cult."

"Well, if that's the case." Bull took her hair down and gazed back at Hemana. "I think it's definitely worth developing them more."

OOPS-A-NAVY

"Admiral—"

"I've made my decision, Ryder. Now I want to get back to your base camp and have an encrypted conversation with Fleet Admiral Kazinski to update him on our progress. The president is getting impatient with us not finding the senator. He's tweeted that we're losers and that he's thinking of abolishing the Department of the Navy." Bull made solid eye contact with Shelby, then Earl too. "But I want you to know that I'm proud of you two doing your duty down here." She extended her arms. "Navy SEAL group hug?"

Shelby knew the Navy SEAL hug being offered by an admiral was a high honor. She spread her arms wide and so did Earl. The three embraced with typical SEAL aggression, butting heads in the middle, and Bull's hands made their way to the back of the two SEAL's necks.

"Ahh," Shelby cried. Bull had so much strength in her hands —unbelievable.

"That hurts, Admiral." Earl frowned.

"Come on, Bernstein." Bull finally released her ironclad grip on their necks. "You need to get over this island-living laziness!"

"Yes, ma'am." Earl rubbed his neck.

"All right now, with no further delay, let's go to your camp— I need to have that conversation with Fleet Admiral Kazinski."

What could Shelby say? Bull going to The Gathering could be a disaster, but she'd issued a direct order. And as nerve-racking as it was having Bull in Candlebrake Cove, it was also stabilizing. They hated her, sure, but to have a clear-thinking patriot, a courageous one, with them really boosted morale. Shelby was focusing more and more on finding Senator Canfield again. The real Senator Canfield. Not the multiple illusory ones. It was time to start living in the real world again. They were Navy SEAL warriors. Not Caribbean Island druggie cult members.

GREGG BELL

* * *

Bull had been in the tent for hours talking to Fleet Admiral Kazinski, and Shelby was loath to interrupt. Dusk and The Gathering with Hemana on the beach were rapidly approaching, and it was looking like they might miss it. Then Shelby thought, maybe that would be all to the good. Bull was already looking spellbound by Hemana. It would be best to nip that sort of thing in the bud, right? Still, Bull was the ranking SEAL in the cove and calling the shots. Finally, though, Shelby made an executive decision to inform Bull that the "beach party" was about to start.

There was no door to the inflatable tent to knock on, so Shelby popped her head in. "Admiral," she called, then she stepped into the tent—and found Bull chugging from the gallon of mushroom smoothie.

"Sorry, Ryder." Bull smiled goofily. "I was parched after talking to Fleet Admiral Kazinski for so long, so I drank some of your milkshake. It's pretty damn good actually." She raised the gallon to her lips and took another long swig.

"No, Admiral!" Shelby rushed to her and snatched the gallon away.

"Well, I'm sorry, Ryder." The rear admiral sounded offended. "I didn't know it was that precious to you."

"No, that's not it, Admiral."

"Well, what then?"

"Oh, you're going to find out very soon."

"Well." Bull straightened her shoulders. "I say, to the beach party."

Oi vey, Shelby thought.

Earl was waiting outside the tent.

When Shelby saw him, she shook her head. "Earl, she drank half a gallon of the mushroom smoothie."

Earl grinned. "This is going to be interesting."

OOPS-A-NAVY

The threesome headed to the beach.

Where Hemana, Talia, the Harringtons and the rest of the group were already gathered around the bonfire. The wind had died down, and the orange clouds reflected their color onto the mirror-smooth cove water. Sparks from the bonfire leapt into the blue-going-purple Caribbean sky.

Bull led the charge. "All righty. We roasting marshmallows here or what? Weenies?" The group had formed a circle, but Bull squeezed in between Hemana and Talia. "We going to tell ghost stories?"

Hemana put a brotherly arm around the rear admiral and smiled. "I can see love already emanating from your essence."

"You bet it is, you buck stud!" She swatted Hemana's bottom. "Hoo boy!"

Shelby and Earl sat between the Harringtons. Shelby was glad to see Hemana and Talia separated, but she was worried about how this would play out for Bull. (She'd never seen Bull under the influence of hallucinogenic drugs before.) She turned to Preston. "Ever see Bull like this?"

"Only once. When Eisenhower won the presidency."

Shelby tilted her head and narrowed her eyes at Bull.

The ceremony proceeded, Hemana making affirmations for universal love and peace, but Bull was getting antsy.

"We could really use some tunes," she said. "Anybody got a radio on 'em?"

Ashley pulled out her phone and plugged in an auxiliary speaker. She played some atmospheric elevator music.

"Oh my God, that's so boring." Bull leaned on Hemana's shoulder. "I feel like I'm gonna pass out."

Hemana reached the point in the service of sharing the mushroom smoothie. "In honor of the great spirit of the universe, we will now partake of the earth's bounty." He held up the silver chalice.

Bull grabbed it. "Ah, more milkshake. I love this stuff." She drank down the whole thing. "Now I can't handle this music. Hey, lady." She eyed Ashley. "You got anything that swings? How about Glenn Miller's 'In the Mood'?"

Ashley did an online search, found the Glenn Miller song and turned up the speaker.

"Now you're talking." Bull jumped up and grabbed Hemana to join her. "C'mon, big boy, I'll show you how to cut a rug!"

Bull was indeed cutting a rug, whirling, twirling. She even did a little breakdancing but found it difficult to spin in the sand. Hemana took a while to get into the swing of things, but now he was dancing too. Bull had him by the hands, swinging her hips and shaking everything she had. Shelby enjoyed watching it all, but her neck was hurting from where Bull had grabbed her (she saw Earl rubbing his neck too) during the Navy SEAL group hug. The woman had the energy and power of a twenty-year-old!

In the distance, Shelby noticed two animals, dark, bounding, darting in front of the woods that surrounded the beach. It was the Komodo dragons that guarded Hemana's second hut. Then, cannibals, their bodies painted like skeleton bones, moved spasmodically along the same path the Komodo dragons had just run.

Shelby grabbed Earl by the elbow. "Did…did you see that?"

"See what?" He frowned and kept rubbing his neck. "I think Bull may have broken a vertebra in my neck."

"At the edge of the trees were cannibals!"

"Sorry, Shelby." He shrugged.

Shelby leaned over. "Ashley, did *you* see them?"

Ashley shook her head.

"Preston?"

"'Fraid not, Shelby."

Earl stood. "Shelby, I really think you have a cannibal phobia. You know, the Navy has a psychiatrist on call 24/7."

OOPS-A-NAVY

"Earl, hurry, look!"

He frowned but looked. "Oh my God."

"So you saw them this time?" Shelby's heart raced.

"Well, I saw *something* that drifted into the woods."

"In the Mood" was ending. Bull finally seemed to be tiring. Shelby knew the massive amount of mushroom smoothie she'd consumed and all her exertion must have been taxing the elderly woman tremendously. But something else came together for Shelby. Earl and her seeing the cannibals, and Preston and Ashley not seeing them told her that it was only those who had imbibed the mushroom smoothie that were seeing things, whether multiple Elvises or Senator Canfields or cannibals or Komodo dragons. The drug was opening up their doors of perception to the vagaries of their unconscious. In other words, this Candlebrake Cove Island Paradise living was a sham. And it was throwing them off the purpose of their mission. What confirmed it were the facts that Senator Canfield was in Cuba to play golf and the only two golf courses were on the other side of the island.

Shelby calmed Bull down so that, along with Earl and the Harringtons, she could be led back to the tent. Upon arrival, Shelby poured out the remaining contents from the gallon of mushroom smoothie. She was taking charge. No more mushroom smoothies for any of them. No more Hemana. (Although she would miss him.) And no more cannibal hallucinations. She radioed the Navy SEAL base in Florida. They would send a transport helicopter to take them all back to Guantanamo in the morning.

Chapter Thirteen

Shelby and Earl, the Harringtons and even Hemana and Talia, were on the beach the next morning as the Navy helicopter rose over the mountains. Hugs were exchanged all around. Bull pleaded to stay and clung to Hemana as the helicopter landed, its rotor wind plastering them with dried seaweed, sand and seashells. Earl cast longing glances at Talia, but hand-in-hand he boarded the chopper with Ashley, and Preston was not far behind. Shelby managed to pry Bull free from Hemana, twisted her arm behind her back, walked her to the chopper and shoved her in. Then once inside, Bull pleaded for a mushroom smoothie for the ride to Guantanamo, but Shelby stayed firm. She knew that when older people got addicted to a drug they went hog-wild. Yes, it was looking like Bull was a magic mushroom addict. And brutal as it might be, she was going to have to go cold turkey to beat her addiction.

Except for Shelby's and Earl's necks hurting from Bull's killer grip during the Navy SEAL group hug, it was a pleasant helicopter ride to Guantanamo. The pilot and his crew were accommodating, serving beverages and light snacks, little bags of honey-coated pretzels and salted peanuts. There wasn't much in the bags, but if they asked for more, the crew happily doled out a few extras.

Bull was whiny about having to leave Hemana. She'd never married (she'd been married to the Navy) and resented having to give up her one chance for wedded bliss. She knew she was past childbearing age but figured they could've adopted. Shelby consoled her as best she could, feeding her pretzels, and just as a precaution locked her seat belt in case the aftereffects of the 'shroom overdose seized her with a desire to jump. ("I can fly!")

OOPS-A-NAVY

They landed directly on Yatera Seca golf course, the indoor-outdoor green mats sent flying in the dust storm kicked up by the chopper's whirling rotors. Shelby wasn't happy about having wasted so much time at Candlebrake Cove, and it was going to be a pain hanging with Bull while she detoxed, but this was a part of what she'd signed on for when she became a SEAL—standing by her fellow SEALs no matter what. Well, at least that's the way she felt most of the time.

The Army grunts at Guantanamo weren't happy about their golf course being so discombobulated, but they dealt with it as best they could, and one of them even carried Bull over his shoulder to the base's medical office.

Doctor Cooke was playing Dungeons and Dragons when they entered. He made them wait ten minutes while he finished the game, then said, "Just throw her up on the exam table."

The grunt did as he was told, fist bumped Shelby and the others and invited them to play Yatera Seca anytime for free, but since it was such a crappy course, and especially after having played the De La Rata course, they all knew it would never be arranged.

Doctor Cooke whipped his long, silvery hair into a ponytail. He smelled nice, some kind of cologne, Shelby thought, for somebody who looked so hippie-like. She, Earl and the Harringtons sat on folding chairs. Dr. Cooke's diplomas and a pretty good pencil sketch of him with shorter hair filled the office walls. Magazines cluttered an end table, but Bull's life hanging in the balance struck them all as being more important than reading year-old copies of *Army* magazine. Actually, they didn't *know* Bull's life hung in the balance, but they felt, well, an eighty-five-year-old overdosing on mushroom smoothies, dancing to the point of exhaustion and then being wrenched away from the man, the he-man, she wanted to marry... Well, that would be enough to make anyone's life hang in the balance.

Dr. Cooke shined a flashlight around Bull's head. "She's got wax buildup in both ears. Does anybody know the last time she cleaned them?"

Heads shook all around. No one knew. How would they? That sort of information was personal.

"There's not that much wax. I can hear you." Bull looked all around. "Where's He-man?"

The doctor turned to the others. "Who's He-man?"

"He's the guy I'm crushin' on." Bull sat up. "And I gotta get back to him before one of those island skanks steals him from me."

Dr. Cooke put his hand on her shoulder. "Admiral Gompers, you need to lie back down."

"Like hell, sonny." She slapped his hand away. "Ever hear the saying, 'You snooze; you lose'? Well, Bull Gomper's never been one to lose."

Again, the doctor turned to the others. "Was she like this on the flight over?"

"Worse," Earl said.

"I've known Bull forty years," Preston added. "And I've never seen her this bad."

"I don't know." Ashley was filing her nails. "She seemed okay to me. She's just stuck on a guy. Happens all the time."

"Well, I'm going with the majority opinion," the doctor said. "I'm giving her something to calm down."

"He-man'll calm me down." Bull started climbing off the exam table. "I can't wait to get my hands on him."

"Hurry, help me keep her up here," Doctor Cooke called to the others.

The three of them rushed to hold Bull down while the doctor gave her an injection.

Boom. She was out.

"Wow, that worked really fast." Earl looked over Bull's limp

OOPS-A-NAVY

body on the exam table.

"Yeah." The doctor sat at his desk, leaned back, put his hands behind his head and feet up. "So, tell me more about her symptoms. I don't usually get such interesting cases. What caused this extreme amount of lust in an eighty-five-year-old woman?"

Shelby wanted to protect Bull's reputation, but the doctor getting accurate medical information was important too. "It was all the drugs she took."

Ashley, sitting next to Earl, slipped her arm around his waist. "I think she just found her soul mate was all."

"Ooh." Earl jumped—maybe he was ticklish. On the other hand, he may have had a slight seizure or it could've been the first sign of Tourette's Syndrome.

The doctor undid his ponytail and lit a cigarette. "What kind of drugs?"

Shelby was embarrassed to even say the words. "Magic mushrooms."

"Ah, psilocybin." The doctor nodded. "I'm familiar with that particular drug. *Very* familiar. Do you happen to have any samples of what she took?"

Bull twitched on the exam table. "He-man," she mumbled.

The group gawked.

"No worries. I gave her enough sedative to knock out a cannibal." The doctor dragged on the cigarette. "Anyway, yes, do you have any samples?"

"No." Shelby gritted her teeth. And why was everybody talking about cannibals? "I threw out what was left of it."

"Hmm." The doctor frowned. "That's too bad."

"But, doctor," Shelby said. "The drug is hallucinatory, isn't it?"

The physician blew out three smoke rings. "That's right."

"Honestly," Shelby continued, "you wouldn't believe the things that happened when Earl and I took it."

"Oh, yes I would. Psilocybin is the most powerful hallucinogenic substance on earth. Try me."

Shelby shuddered.

Earl whispered in her ear, "Go ahead. Tell him."

"Off the record, doc?" Shelby caught his eye. Her career was on the line.

"That's fine."

Shelby went for it. "Doctor, I've seen things you wouldn't believe. Attack ships on fire off the shoulder of Orion. I watched C-beams glitter in the dark—"

Earl elbowed her. "No, that's from *Blade Runner*."

"Oh." Shelby blushed. "That's right. (I'm still a bit under the drug's influence myself.) But we did see amazing things. Multiple Senator Canfields and Komodo dragons."

"I saw multiple Elvises." Earl seemed excited to contribute to the conversation.

"Yeah." Shelby felt better getting this stuff off her chest. "And, doc, I *really* felt like I saw those things."

"It's not unusual." The doctor stubbed out his cigarette and took a bite out of a Twinkie. "That's why they call them hallucinations."

"Doctor." Shelby was getting really emotional. It was the same level of emotional intensity she'd felt the first time she beat her sister playing ping-pong. "I felt like I was in two places at the same time!"

The doctor talked with his mouth full of the Twinkie. "Happens with psilocybin regularly."

Shelby's breathing quickened. "I saw cannibals!"

"Not unusual."

"No kidding?" Shelby's breathing started slowing, becoming more regulated. "Oh, thank you, doctor, because I really thought I might be losing my mind."

"He-man. He-man." Bull twitched on the table. "Ready or

not, big boy. Here comes mama!"

"That's really unsettling." Earl looked away from Bull and grimaced.

"That's just the way octogenarians act on the drug." The doctor stood. "Look, I have to do some electroshock therapy, so I'm not going to be able to chat with you all much longer."

Preston stood too. "Electroshock therapy? On Bull?"

"Of course, on Bull." The doctor put his hand in his pocket and pulled out a breath mint. "The old girl needs help. We need to rid her of those memories of He-man or she won't be able to carry out her duties."

"It's Hema*na* actually." Shelby was wondering if she herself would be able to function without him.

"Whatever." The physician tossed the breath mint in the air and caught it in his mouth.

"Well, doctor," Preston said. "I suppose you're right. Just don't overdo it."

"Nah, 50,000 volts ten or twelve times will knock this He-man nonsense right out of her."

Shelby was relieved. She gave the doctor a hug. "It's good to know you'll be looking out for her."

* * *

Shelby, Earl and the Harringtons left Doctor Cooke's office and stood in the humid ninety-degree heat. Night would soon be coming on. They felt that what they'd been through together was amazing, and they were reluctant to part. Friendships made under duress were often the best friendships SEALs had. Well, actually, they were the only ones they had since the life of a SEAL was a life of duress. They exchanged hugs (Earl's hug of Ashley was extremely gropey), and then the Harringtons called a limo to take them to De La Rata Country Club, while Earl and Shelby said they'd be okay walking to their tent in the jungle.

"It's hard to leave Bull, isn't it, Earl?" Shelby was getting sentimental. "It's amazing the old gal is still alive. She's a fighter. You have to give her that much."

"I guess, but if she dies, at least we won't be de-SEALed."

"You got a point there."

"So what about weapons?" Earl nodded. "We've gone so long without any, I've almost forgotten what it's like to have them."

"That's true. A SEAL without weaponry is like a TV without an electrical outlet."

"I never heard that one before."

"Really? I hear it all the time."

"So, want to stop at the garrison and pick up some machine guns?" Earl's eyes were bloodshot. It could just be that he was tired or it could be the poison-drug blow dart, the magic mushroom smoothie, malaria or tiny ocular pulmonary embolisms.

"You know what?" Shelby flapped her arms against her sides like a penguin. "I think we don't need them. Especially since all the dangers we've faced so far have been hallucinatory. And it'll be more of a challenge to our survival skills to get through whatever is coming up without them. I say we just pick up a couple of machetes so we can hack our way back to the tent."

"Okay." Earl laughed. "We don't need any stinkin' weapons! But we better hurry because it'll be dark soon."

"So let's go."

They walked through Guantanamo's razor-wire-topped gate and shuffled along dusty Cuban streets.

"Hey look." Earl pointed. "There's a street peddler."

A Cuban guy wearing a NY Yankees baseball cap was leaning on a vending cart. It looked like he was ready to call it a day. His cart was loaded with single-serving bottles of apple juice

OOPS-A-NAVY

from concentrate, tamales, hand sanitizer, lottery tickets and machetes.

Seeing the selection of machetes had Shelby's eyes popping. Machete shopping was always fun for SEALs, especially female SEALs, the men not so much as they were more interested in weapons that blew things up. There were shiny-bladed machetes, black steel ones with serrated edges, rusty ones, all kinds.

The peddler said something in Spanish like "Oprah." Maybe he'd been watching TV.

"Yeah, pal." Earl hardly knew any Spanish but figured he could wing it. "*Requesto machetes por favor.*"

The peddler rolled his eyes but said, "*Si.*"

"I'd like an apple juice too, Earl." Shelby hadn't had apple juice since she'd been in Kansas.

"Okay." Earl turned back to the guy. "*How mucho por los machetes?*"

"Oooh." Shelby pointed. "I like that one with the skull and crossbones on the handle."

"Yeah, that one's a beaut." Earl snatched it. "*Okayo, this uno and this uno,*" he said as he grabbed something that was more similar in shape to a sickle. He handed the evil-looking machete to Shelby and looked at the peddler. "*How mucho?*"

The man pushed the dusty earth around with his boot. "One hundred US dollars."

"Ha ha ha." Earl knew that was too much. Now he was hoping the guy wouldn't get Shelby angry. Price gouging was one of her pet peeves. "*Too mucho, amigo.* I'll give you ten. And you'll have to throw in a couple of bottles of apple juice." He pulled out a sawbuck.

"No." The guy plucked the sickle back, but Shelby already had the evil-looking machete firmly in hand.

"*Pal-o, por favor, usted don't want her to go loco.*"

Shelby whirled the machete so fast it sliced through a leg of

123

the peddler's cart, and it was done so rapidly the leg still stood.

"*Si, si, si!*" The guy grabbed the money and handed over the sickle and two juices.

"*Gracias.*" Shelby saluted him with the machete.

They headed into the jungle.

"You know." Earl drank some apple juice. "I think that was a fair deal, don't you?"

Shelby thrashed the machete, chopping down a banana tree. "Absolutely. The guy was trying to make us overpay just because we're from the United States. And then they turn around and call *us* Ugly Americans."

"I never did understand that." Earl screwed the cap on his apple juice—he wanted to save some for before he went to sleep. "I don't think we're any uglier than people from other countries."

"I think we're better-looking."

They made it to the tent. It was still inflated so that was good, but it had been bombed with parrot droppings. They settled in and Earl drank what was left of his apple juice and brushed his teeth.

Shelby felt a terrible void in her heart where Hemana had been. She also felt not a little jealous of the way Earl groped every woman in sight (well, except for Bull). "Earl, you really are the horniest guy, aren't you?"

He plopped down on his side of the tent. "Yeah, I guess that's true."

She sucked in a quick breath. "But…but do you ever think you could control it? I mean, do you think if a woman really loved you, you could love her back and settle down?"

He scratched his head. "Nah."

Shelby sighed. Oh well. She knew that was coming. She kicked off her boots. "So it was pretty nutty back there at Candlebrake Cove, the mushroom smoothies and all?"

"Oh, yeah."

"Do you think Bull will ever get her right mind back?"

OOPS-A-NAVY

He shrugged. "I think it's possible. But she drank five times as much as we did."

"Earl?"

"What?"

She missed Hemana, yes, but she was thinking maybe Earl could fill the void, even if it wasn't the real thing, at least for tonight. She would give the world just to be held. "Nothing."

"Well, go to sleep." He pulled mosquito netting over himself.

"Earl?"

"What, Shelby?" he asked, an edge in his voice now.

She hesitated, then said, "Remember when you faced down the crocodile in the swamp for me?"

He said nothing. She imagined he was remembering his heroism and too manly to claim credit.

Finally he said, "No."

"Oh!" The inescapable reality that he was still Earl was coming back to her. "How could you not remember something like that? The boa constrictor had my leg, and you were trying to drown it so it would release me, and then the croc swam up, and you jumped into the swamp and stared it down."

"Well." He yawned. "I guess it's vaguely familiar now that you're supplying some details."

"Oh my God."

"Why?"

She was just lonely. Really lonely. She swallowed hard. "Do you think...do you think maybe you could come over to my side of the tent tonight?"

"Really?" A reawakened lust was all over his voice.

"Not for that. But if you could just hold me till I fall asleep. But you'd have to promise you won't do anything more—once I drift off, you'll just go back to your side."

He groaned. "What if I can't make that promise?"

"Earl! For God's sake, can't you be a nice guy for once in

your life?"

He shrugged and lifted the mosquito netting. "I don't know, Shelby. If I'm nice, what is that going to do to your image of me as a smokin' hot Navy SEAL stud?"

She laughed and felt the inflated tent wobbling underneath her as he padded across the floor.

Chapter Fourteen

In the morning Shelby was back to her alpha-female Navy SEAL warrior pile-driving self. But she did have sweet memories of Earl holding her last night as she drifted off to sleep. It seemed he actually had some good in him, but she didn't want him thinking she might be attracted to him. Not that he might be attracted to her, with him lusting for Ashley and Talia and half the females on the island. And yeah, it was true, Hemana would've been a good partner for her. But a relationship with him wasn't practical. She'd probably have to move down here as she couldn't see him moving to Kansas. And anyway, it was time to put God and country or country and God, or whatever that saying was, first. She was a SEAL, damnit! She had a mission. Especially now that Bull was out of action and near death.

Earl was brushing his teeth. He was upset because his electric toothbrush's charge was running low, so its bristles weren't whirling as fast as they normally did. He figured his teeth were proportionately becoming that much more susceptible to enamel erosion. Not that he had much choice about it. He hadn't been near an electrical outlet in so long to charge it. He too recalled pleasant memories of last night as he made sure to get the toothbrush in good behind those back molars. Last night he'd been tempted. Oh, yes, he'd been tempted to let his hands wander over Shelby's slightly overweight but still luscious body after she'd fallen asleep in his arms. Okay, okay, so his hands had accidentally drifted where they shouldn't have a couple of times, but still, he'd been a real stand-up guy.

Shelby was all business. She swiped on underarm deodorant. (It was just deodorant, not antiperspirant. She figured it was a good thing for a SEAL, especially a female SEAL, to show that she sweats.) She ate a banana, grabbed her machete and was ready to go. "Earl." She made sure she had his eye. "We are on a mission to find the senator and nothing else. I haven't gone through all this Navy SEAL training, Hell Week and all, to be de-SEALed, so let's make a pact to find Senator Canfield or die."

Earl spat out his anti-cavity rinse. "What do you mean 'die'? You mean that figuratively, right?"

"No, Earl. I mean die die."

He screwed the cap back on the rinse bottle, wondering if he'd have enough while he was down there, and if he ran out, did Cuban peddlers sell anti-cavity rinse? His brand? Reasonably priced? "Shelby, I think 'die die' is a little extreme. It's fine for motivational purposes, but I plan on living longer than my great-grandma Miriam, so I would have to say 'die die' isn't realistic."

"Well, how old is your great-grandma?"

"A hundred and two."

"And *that's* realistic?!"

He half-smiled. "Shelby, the average male life expectancy is growing exponentially. Some of these Silicon Valley tech guys are talking about living forever."

"Oh, Earl." She rubbed her neck. "We're digressing. How 'bout we just say we'll do our best, our absolute best, to get the senator?"

"I can live with that."

"Okay, grab your machete and let's go. We're off to De La Rata Golf Course."

They set out. The heat of the morning sun blazed down. Monkeys screeched in the interconnected banyan tree branches and vines above that created a wondrous cathedral-like natural vault. Back on the ground, though, Shelby was thinking this wasn't the safest-looking stretch of jungle she'd been in. Maybe it would've been better if they *had* gotten weapons from the Guantanamo garrison before they'd left.

OOPS-A-NAVY

"Hey, Shelby, what's that?" Earl pointed with his sickle at a bush that seemed to be moving.

Shelby for a split-second thought maybe it was still the aftereffects of the mushroom smoothies distorting their perception. She'd had enough of being dazed and confused by the hallucinogen. But none of that mattered anymore because before she knew it, a host (well maybe not a host but nine or ten anyway) of rainforest savages swung down on vines and stood with their legs wide blocking the path. It took a while, but the more Shelby looked at them, the more they seemed familiar. "Hey, aren't you the same guys who stopped us before?"

The savage with the dried-grass hat seemed to be the leader. "Yes, this is our 'hood."

Earl whispered in Shelby's ear, "I think we gave them the Scrabble game—I wish we hadn't."

"You gave us faulty board game in exchange for passage," the leader said, some of his buds grunting their agreement, thumping the ground with the flat ends of their spears.

"Faulty how?" Earl asked. "The game was in perfect condition when we gave it to you."

The leader brushed his hand through his dried-grass hat and looked down. "Well, maybe not faulty, but over time we lost all the little wood chips with the strange symbols on them."

"You mean the letters," Shelby corrected, trying to be helpful. (She'd always been an advocate of improving the lives of third-world inhabitants in any way she could.)

"Are you making fun of Chief?" He brandished his spear.

"No, sorry, Chief." Shelby really was sorry. He being third world and all and wearing that silly dried-grass hat that he surely must think was stylish.

"Shelby," Earl said basically as an aside. "Remember, our mission is to get the senator or die."

Shelby nodded. "But I thought you weren't agreeing to the

die part?"

"Well, I wasn't." Earl sighed. "I guess I'm just a little unsure about running into these savages again."

Another of the savages, a guy with very creative body paint and a nice pair of orange surfer trunks (Shelby and Earl both wondered where they all got surfer trunks from) seemed upset. "Do not call us savages."

Earl saw an opening. "What do you prefer to be called?"

The savage seemed bewildered. "I don't know. I guess we haven't thought about it much. Just not savages."

Fair enough, Earl thought. "That's doable. Isn't it, Shelby?"

"Absolutely." But Earl was right—they needed to find the senator. If they didn't, Bull Gompers might de-SEAL them as soon as she came to from Dr. Cooke's knocking her out with the sedative. And then there was the likelihood of a nuclear war too. "All right, people, what do we have to do to get by this time?"

The leader conferred with the others. He emerged from the huddle. "We want your machete and the uh…the uh…" He pointed.

Earl held up the sickle. "It's called a sickle."

"Okay," said the leader. "The machete and the sickle."

Shelby didn't see the logic in this. "But we need to get to the golf course and how will we hack our way out of the jungle without the machete and sickle?"

The leader pushed his chest out and pointed toward the golf course. "We will show you secret passage—no hacking necessary."

Shelby looked at Earl. "Sounds fair to me. What do you think?"

"It was really hard hacking with the sickle anyway, so yeah, I say let's do it."

"All right, Chief, you've got a deal." Shelby lofted her machete toward him and it landed gently at his feet.

OOPS-A-NAVY

Earl followed suit, but his sickle bounced on the hard earth and nicked the chief's big toe, sending the savage hopping around on one foot, like he was doing a Mexican rain dance, which would've made sense had they been in Mexico. "Sorry, sorry. My bad, Chief."

"That's it!" cried the chief, no longer hopping at this point. He seemed bent on revenge. "Subdue them!"

"Wait, wait." Shelby held up both palms. "It's only a scratch, Chief. Just put a little Neosporin on it. Subduing us is definitely overreacting."

But the savages subdued them anyway by tying them on bamboo stretchers, and carried them to their hideaway.

* * *

Shelby was growing unhappy about all this even if these were indigenous people from whom the white man had taken away their way of life, tomahawk and the bow and knife. The savages set the stretchers they'd bound them on at forty-five-degree angles, and women and little savages came out of the surrounding huts to ogle them. "I don't know about you, Earl, but I've just about had it with these savages. We gave them Scrabble. We tried to be nice. Now by subduing us, they've crossed a line."

"I'm with you on that." Earl wrinkled his nose, trying to shoo a fly crawling across his cheek. With his luck, he was thinking, it was probably a tsetse fly. "And this could keep us from finding the senator and get us de-SEALed."

"Yeah, and there'll be a nuclear war. That wouldn't be good either."

Okay, here came the chief and the savages. They were carrying two machetes each (Shelby noticed one of the chief's machetes had the skull and crossbones on it) and chafing them against one another as if they were sharpening them. Which made sense because a dull machete was useless when it came to hacking through the jungle.

"Shelby?" Earl was looking off to the side. Two poles were anchored in the hard dirt ground, a rope strung between them. And dangling from the rope were other ropes that seemed to hold —Earl got a little sick to his stomach—shriveled human heads. "Look to your left."

Shelby hardly had time to look anywhere as the machete-sharpening savages closed in, but she took a quick gander. "Is that...is that what I think it is?"

"Uh-huh."

"These savages are actually...cannibals?!"

"Yep." Earl closed his eyes. He'd been thinking this whole being subdued experience would give him awesome material for writing his next poem, but the cannibalism angle provided a whole new perspective to the savages' machete sharpening, and he was concerned.

The savages were upon them.

"Wait wait wait!" Shelby cried. "You've got this all wrong."

The chief raised his machete to decapitate her, but he stopped at the last second. "What do you mean we've got it all wrong?"

"Well, I mean, you're going to eat the two of us skinny people when we can lead you to a gourmet meal of a hundred overweight Germans?"

"You are not so skinny," the chief said, grabbing one of her love handles and then made as if to resume the decapitation blow.

"Maybe not, Chief, but you should see these German tubbies! You'd have enough to feed your whole village for a year, hell, a year and a half!" Still, she wasn't happy about the chief's snarky comment about her weight. She'd remember that no matter how this turned out.

"Really?" The chief lowered the machete.

"Yes! You'll be able to store mountains of sausage-fed

OOPS-A-NAVY

German blubber in your storehouses for years."

The chief sneered and waved the machete dismissively. "How could we store blubber for years? The blubber we have only lasts a few days in this tropical heat."

"That's easy, Chief. You salt it."

"Salt it?"

"Yeah. You go down to the ocean and bring back seawater and then let the water evaporate and the result is sea salt. (It's healthier than table salt.) You then salt the blubber, and the blubber keeps for years. If you want, I can walk you through it."

The savage with the orange surfer trunks spoke up. "These white dogs are lying just like the Spanish dogs lied to our ancestors centuries ago. We must kill and eat them. You know what our elders always said, 'a body on the plate is better than several in the bush.'"

Earl was taking mental notes. So that's where that saying came from!

"There are no Germans on the island," the orange-trunked one continued. "No, we must kill and eat them now."

The chief seemed to be getting won over by that argument. "Yes, there are no Germans on the island."

"Hoh, are you kidding me, Chief?" Shelby knew this might be her last chance. "There is a huge traveling tuba-playing Oktoberfest band touring the island. And I can show you *exactly* where they are."

Earl whispered to Shelby, "Could those Germans be the same Germans as the tuba band Elvis was conducting at Candlebrake Cove?"

"Earl, I'm making this up," Shelby said between gritted teeth.

The chief scratched his dried-grass hat with the butt handle of his machete. "I don't know."

"I can. Trust me." Shelby smiled confidently. "Hey, didn't we give you the Scrabble game in good faith?"

The chief nodded. "But we lost all the pieces."

"Well, that wasn't our fault, was it, Chief?" She could sense him weakening.

"No, I guess not." He lowered the machete to his side.

"Kill them!" the orange-trunked one demanded.

The guy was getting on Earl's nerves, but his Navy SEAL patience kicked in. It came to him. He had a game of checkers back at the tent—with magnetic pieces so they wouldn't be lost! It was a perfect fit. "Easy does it there, Gunga Din. I've got an idea. You don't eat us, and we'll give you another board game. This one's called Checkers, and I think you'll like it a lot. And as a bonus, you'll be less likely to lose the pieces!"

The savages crossed their arms over their wildly painted chests and brooded over the offers.

The chief addressed Shelby again. "Where are these Germans? If they are in Havana or another city, we cannot get them as we stand out in places like that."

"They're not in any city, Chief." Shelby wasn't so sure she had him anymore. "They're practicing their tuba playing in the jungle *before* they go into the city."

"Where in the jungle?" The chief seemed to be coming around.

"By the Great Waterfall."

The chief scratched his nose. "There is no waterfall in the jungle."

"Kill them!" The orange-trunked one again. "Besides, I'm getting hungry."

When the chief turned to him and said, "Go eat your fill of bananas and coconuts," Shelby knew she had him!

"Oh, but there is a waterfall, Chief. True, it's in a secret place, but I can lead you there." Ha ha. She might be from Kansas, but she knew how to talk her way out of a jam.

Again, the chief seemed to be thinking, puffing his cheeks,

OOPS-A-NAVY

tightening his lips. "Okay, you will lead us to the tubby Germans."

"Awesome!" Shelby blew out a deep exhalation. "You won't regret this, Chief." But really, especially considering that snarky comment he'd made about her weight, if she had anything at all to say about things, eventually he was going to very much regret it.

"Give her coconut milk and fresh oranges." Then the chief turned to Earl. "Him, kill and fry up for lunch."

"Wait! Hey! Shelby!" Earl was quite disturbed by what he'd just heard.

Shelby actually had thought Earl was a part of the deal. Now she'd just about run out of creative thinking. Really, the important thing was fulfilling the mission anyway, and ever since Earl had been struck by the poison-drug blow dart, he'd been a substantial burden and jeopardized it. And he's always so horny, groping anything female that moves. No, this might be the end for him. One of the savages held up a half-shell coconut with a straw and Shelby drank the cool coconut milk.

"Shelby, do something!"

"I'm thinking, Earl." She took another sip. "Thank you," she said to the savage. "It's really refreshing, especially in this heat."

"Shelby!!"

"Okay, okay, cool your jets. I got this."

The orange-trunked savage was back after eating something, but apparently he was still hungry because he put his machete to Earl's throat and grinned from ear to ear.

"Wait just a second, cowboy," Shelby said. She turned to the chief. "Chief, stop him for a minute."

The chief held up his hand, and the savage lowered the machete, but just an inch.

"Chief, if you eat Bernstein, you'll be eating the poison-drug you put in him when you hit him with the blow dart." Shelby caught his eye and nodded. "Uh-huh?"

The chief rubbed his neck. "Hmm. I suppose you're right."

"Yes, Chief, and besides, I need him because he speaks German, and that'll come in handy when we trick the fat Germans into being cannibalized."

Thoroughly won over by that logic, the chief said, "That makes sense. Spare them both."

Chapter Fifteen

The savages carried Earl and Shelby on the stretchers through the jungle, Shelby barking directions now and then.

"Shelby, that was really close back there." Earl felt as if he'd almost bought the farm, and what a way that would've been to go. He saw the headlines in his mind's eye: NAVY SEAL EATEN FOR LUNCH. And his parents would be saying to each other: "He never should have left home. He should've listened to us and become a proctologist."

"What about me, Earl?" Shelby was glad they didn't have to walk—it was nice being carried. "Cannibals are my biggest fear, and I thought they only existed in my imagination because of the mushroom smoothies."

"Yeah, I guess it wasn't easy for either of us." Earl looked up at the forest canopy and thought there must be a poem in this somehow. A burst of inspiration hit. *Nearly eaten for lunch / I stare up at bunch after bunch / of bananas in the arching jungle vault / my situation hardly my fault.* "Can I tell you a poem that just came to me?"

"This probably isn't a good time."

Earl sighed. His stretcher was making his butt itch, but he had no way of scratching it. "Hopefully I can commit it to memory because it would be a shame to lose this one."

Shelby sensed the vegetation becoming thinner—a sure sign they were approaching the end of the jungle. This would be a tricky juncture.

The savages stopped. The chief got in her face. "We are at end of jungle and there is no waterfall." He scowled. "White dogs! Now you will die!"

"Chief, Chief, Chiefffff." Shelby sounded a soothing tone—

she knew being aggressive would be counterproductive. "The Great Waterfall *is* there. In fact, it's only a few feet away. But you need to release me, so I can lead you the final steps because I can't see where we're going."

The orange-trunked savage came up to Earl's stretcher. "Enough of this charade. I say, kill them!"

Earl's eyes widened. 'Charade.' He was impressed with the savage's vocabulary. But still, the savage's belligerence was getting to him. "Uh, it's not a charade, pal."

Shelby murmured, "Earl, let me handle this."

What could he say? Ah, maybe it was for the best—she did get him out of that last predicament.

"Think, Chief." Shelby smiled. "Two skinny—well, okay, you don't think I'm so skinny—Americans or a hundred tubby Germans?"

The chief seemed antsy. He tapped the butt of his spear on the ground. Finally, he turned to his buds. "Okay, unbind the woman!"

"What about me?" Earl nodded.

"Him kill!" the chief ordered.

"Uh-uh-uh." Shelby craned her neck to catch the Chief's eye. "Remember, I need him because he speaketh the *Deutsch*."

The chief frowned but ordered Earl released, as well.

Hmm, Shelby thought, now comes the hard part. The huge fountain—the Great Waterfall to the savages—fronted the De La Rata Country Club. She needed to convince the savages to walk a half mile or so on golf course property, where they might encounter non-savages (golfers). She instinctively knew this might be troubling to them, but to ease their discomfort she had a plan. "All right, you guys, listen up."

"Me too?" Earl asked. "Or just them?"

Shelby was sure the poison-drug blow dart was still affecting him. She shook her head, then said to the savages, "The Great

OOPS-A-NAVY

Waterfall is very near. At the top of it are the tubby Germans. All you have to do is follow me and I will take you to them."

The savages seemed okay with that. Until they got to the edge of the country club parking lot.

"This is the evil land," the chief said, holding the sides of his head as if someone was blowing an air horn next to it. "The land of the white devil." He turned to Shelby. "You said the Great Waterfall was in jungle."

Shelby nodded and tried her best to sound contrite. "I know I did, Chief, but I also knew that if you could get out of your comfort zone just a little, you would be able to feast on the fat Germans. Yes, Chief, I told you a white lie, but I only did it for your sake."

Earl rolled his eyes.

"So what do you say, Chief?" Shelby nodded encouragingly. "Think of all the squaws and little Chiefs back at camp being able to eat obese Germans for years to come."

The chief grunted and then shrugged.

"Chief?"

"Okay, okay," he said gruffly. "But we can go like this?" He held out his arms as if to put himself on display.

Shelby tried to break it to him gently. "Well, not exactly, but a few things are working for you."

The chief waited, his face going red. In the jungle he was king. Out of it, he was…not king. "What do we need to do?"

"Okay, like I said, a few things are working for you." She caught his eye. "Can you line the guys up so we can do this efficiently?"

The chief said something to the savages in their native tongue, and they lined up.

"Nice. Okay." Shelby looked them over like a drill instructor inspecting a regiment. "Now being so near the ocean, it's awesome that you guys are all wearing surfer trunks."

The savages looked down at their trunks and nodded.

"But the rest of it…" Shelby shook her head. "…needs serious help."

The chief seemed offended. "What kind of help?"

"Well." She looked at his dried-grass hat. "For starters—I'm sorry, Chief, personally I like it, but for the country club set it just doesn't work—your hat has to go."

He touched his hat as if it were a crown. "But this shows I am chief!"

"Well, you'll still be chief." She took the hat off his head and laid it on one of the stretchers. "But trust me, for a few minutes—before you feast on the roly-poly Germans—you're all going to need to be surfers."

The chief's brow furrowed.

"Yes, Chief, surfers." Really, he didn't look himself without the hat, but she figured she'd get used to him without it in time. "The guys who ride waves. You know. Surf's up. Surfin' Safari. All that."

"Oh." The chief nodded. "The Beach Boys."

"Riiiiight!" Shelby fist bumped him. "Okay, and all the headbands, necklaces and especially the spears need to go too."

The savages grumbled, but they removed their headgear, then set their spears in a big pile.

"Lastly." Shelby was feeling good about their compliance. In fact, sometimes they didn't even seem all that savage and she considered thinking of them as indigenous again. "As much as I personally like it, you're going to have to get rid of the body war paint. Now there…" She pointed. "…are some papayas growing. The juice is good for removing the tree-root concoction you painted yourself with."

Nobody was happy about this, but the indigenous sensing a big meal were now putty in Shelby's hands. Off came the war paint.

OOPS-A-NAVY

"I gotta tell you guys," Shelby continued, "I know you have your native cultural traditions you want to preserve and I commend that, but, dudes, this is a good look for you."

The indigenous seemed to enjoy the compliment, looking each other over admiringly.

Shelby gave Earl a knowing look before turning back to the indigenous.

"Okay, you could really use having some flip-flops, but you're looking good." She smiled at them. "Now one final thing, if anyone happens to stop us—and I don't anticipate this happening—you guys just say things like: 'rad,' 'dude,' 'surf's up,' or 'shoot the curl,' and most importantly, call each other and whomever you might talk to 'bro.'"

The indigenous tried out the new words. Earl coached the guys that struggled. And Shelby was thinking this might actually work. All that was left was the execution.

"All right, bros," Shelby said, eliciting a chuckle from the indigenous. "Here we go."

They ventured out of the jungle. It was only a stone's throw to reach the country club's fountain (the Great Waterfall). Yes, Shelby knew certain things worked against them, especially that all the indigenous, and Earl for that matter, had jet-black hair and no surfboards, but they were playing ball as best they could, calling each other "bro," and really she couldn't ask for anything more. The one thing she hadn't thought of was what she and Earl were going to do when they got to the top of the fountain. For certainly, when the indigenous saw no fat Germans there, they would be disappointed, disillusioned and could be angry.

Okay, they were in the golf course parking lot. Shelby rationalized that the golfers would just think that the "surfers" were taking a shortcut to the ocean. She knew it was a stretch, but hey, she had to hang on to something. As a few golf carts rolled into the parking lot, some of the indigenous waved to the golfers.

So far so good.

Now they were at the base of the huge fountain, and Shelby gave Earl another knowing look.

"What's that look supposed to mean?" Earl seemed miffed. "You keep shooting me these looks and I don't know what they mean."

Shelby didn't know what the look meant either, but things were happening too fast to try to explain. On the far side of the parking lot, a golf cart transporting the Harringtons entered! Oh no! Please don't see us! She turned away and lowered her head.

But Earl called out, waving his arms, "Hey, Ashley, Preston, over here!"

Oh Lord, here they come. "Okay," Shelby told the indigenous. "These are friends of ours, so please just be cool." Shelby didn't want the Harringtons being eaten on her conscience.

"Hey, Shelby and Earl," Ashley said. "Who are your friends?"

"Shoot the curl, bro," the chief said.

Oh, this wasn't going to work, Shelby thought. She felt bad about what she was about to do, but she had to get the Harringtons out of there for their own good. "Piss off, Ashley! You too, Preston!"

The Harringtons' faces fell. Preston said, "What? What's going on?"

Earl grabbed Shelby by the arm. "You're being rude!"

Shelby punched him in the gut and he doubled over. Meanwhile, the Harringtons, aghast, cleared out of there in a hurry. Okay, Shelby thought, now it was just her, Earl and the indigenous, who seemed a little confused by her slugging Earl. The situation was still dangerous, yes, but at least there wasn't the added pressure of the Harringtons being eaten. (If she lived, Shelby figured she could patch things up with them later, say she had her period or something.)

They made their way up alongside the fountain. The water poured down like from Niagara Falls (well, not that much of course but a lot), slamming into the first pool, then rushing over the edge of that pool and dropping into the next one and likewise down the seven pools all the way to the bottom. They only had a few more steps to reach the top, where Shelby had promised the indigenous the Germanic obese tuba players would be. She could see the growing expectation in their eyes.

They breached the top and to Shelby's surprise the De La Rata Grill, the country club's swank outdoor restaurant, was loaded with fat diners! Shelby didn't know if they were Germans —it was unlikely though—but she figured the indigenous thought they were! So in that sense she felt better because she'd, to a degree anyway, fulfilled her promise to them. But still, she didn't want the diners being eaten either. She looked at the chief. He was rubbing his hands together in culinary anticipation. He yelled, "Surf's up!" and ran toward the diners. The other indigenous joined him.

Oh God! Shelby yelled, "Run! Cannibals!"

Certainly most, if not all, of the diners were exceedingly surprised, especially since the De La Rata Grill was quite exclusive (gratuities of 30% were automatically included in the bill), but the state of the world being what it was, the diners also knew terrorists could strike anywhere. (Though to be fair to the diners, they might've been expecting bombs but certainly not cannibals.) Fortunately, though, they heeded Shelby's warning and hightailed it into the country club.

Which left Shelby and Earl alone with the indigenous, who, Shelby had to admit were, despite looking a little like surfers, looking more and more like savages again. The veins throbbing in their necks. Their eyes burning with hate.

Shelby turned to Earl. "What do you think we should do?"

"Didn't you plan for what will happen now?"

"Well no actually, but I think I did pretty good getting us this far."

The savages ran at them.

Shelby retained enough composure to grab Earl by his good arm, run with him to the edge of the fountain, and then leap into the top pool. At first they thought they were safe. (Thinking it doubtful the savages could swim.) But the savages came plummeting over the edge and landed like depth charges, one savage's foot even clonking Earl in the head. So Shelby and Earl went over the ledge into the next pool, but the pesky savages followed. Knowing they had the advantage of their SEAL training and that they could swim faster, they went over each of the seven levels to the base of the fountain (or as the savages thought of it: The Great Waterfall).

When Shelby looked back at the fountain, the savages were reaching the sixth pool. They'd be on them shortly. She looked around. No way! That little Cuban bicycle-taxi driver with the handlebar mustache came pedaling by. Shelby ran out, Earl following, and stopped him.

"Manuel! Manuel! Do you remember me?"

The little Cuban looked uncertain. "Kind of. Maybe if you weren't all wet."

"I'm the Navy SEAL. You massaged my feet."

A glimmer of recognition dawned in his eyes. "Okay, I think I remember you."

"We slept together in the tent in the jungle!"

"You slept with him?!" Earl clenched his fists.

"Oh, I didn't sleep with him, sleep with him, Earl." Was he actually jealous? She looked at The Great Waterfall (even she was thinking of it as that at this point) as the chief and the better swimmers among them were emerging from the seventh pool. (Shelby thought they swam remarkably well, all things

OOPS-A-NAVY

considered.)

"Manuel, you have to take us!" Shelby nodded pleadingly.

"Wait a minute. Wait a minute." Manuel looked at Earl. "He's the guy who body-slammed me into the sand trap. Forget it."

Shelby got in his face. "But he apologized."

"Well, that's true, but even so, my kidneys still hurt."

"Manuel." Shelby pulled out a handful of soggy cash. "We'll pay you triple your normal fare."

"Triple. Really?" Manuel looked them over. "But you're all wet. You'll mess up my sidecar." He rose up in his bicycle seat to look over their shoulders. "Who are those guys running toward us?"

"Cannibals!"

"Cannibals! Holy crap! Hop in!"

*　　*　　*

Manuel was pedaling hard, looking over his shoulder at the cannibals chasing them. He glanced at Shelby and Earl in the sidecar. "Where to?!"

Shelby and Earl also were keeping an eye on the cannibals. "Anywhere!" Shelby yelled.

"All right, then!" Manuel put his head down and churned his little Cuban legs.

He drove them out to a hillside filled with ramshackle houses and lean-tos, some brick, some wood, most with corrugated tin roofs. When the grade of the dirt hill became too steep, he stopped pedaling and jumped off the bicycle taxi. "My muscles were cramping, and I was afraid I was going to have a heart attack, so we have to walk from here."

Shelby and Earl climbed out of the sidecar and stretched their legs.

Shelby said, "What's this place?"

"This is where I live." Manuel pushed the bicycle taxi up the road. "Feel free to help."

Shelby jumped right in, but Earl had a dazed look on his face.

"I'd help, but a poem is coming to me." Now he had to try it out on them. A poem without an audience was like the sound of one hand clapping in the forest. "Here it is. *We had seemed beat / Shelby and I, us the cannibals soon to eat / But a little Cuban materialized just at the right moment on his bike / And stuck his finger in the proverbial dike*." He chuckled.

Manuel groaned, but when he looked at Earl said, "I liked it. But I'm thinking the ending was a little highbrow for my sensibility."

Hmm, Earl thought. He hadn't been expecting such a learned critique. "Nice. Thanks."

"Now if you don't mind." Manuel nodded for him to pitch in pushing.

"Of course." Earl joined them. "But I was thinking of changing that last line to: *And then up a hill they took a hike*."

"That's better." Manuel coughed. "But now the cadence is off."

"Oh, okay." Earl kept thinking of alternative endings. He was excited to have someone with taste giving him feedback. This could really help him develop as a poet.

They arrived at Manuel's. He chained the bicycle taxi to a pole.

"I'm sorry we got the sidecar all wet," Shelby said. "The cushions should dry out in a day or two, though."

"Yeah, okay," Manuel said, but he seemed distracted.

Earl raised a forefinger. "I've got it: *Saved by the little pedaling tyke*."

Manuel sighed but said, "There you go. You nailed it."

"The cadence too?"

"Oh yeah. Everything."

OOPS-A-NAVY

Earl hugged Manuel. "Thanks, bro."

Shelby could see the surfer talk they'd coached the cannibals to use had influenced Earl as well. Manuel's dwelling was a brick building. A shirtless black Cuban guy in yellow shorts that hung low exposing several inches of his royal-blue boxer shorts stood watching them from the rooftop terrace of the adjacent building. Shelby was a little creeped out. "Who's the black guy, Manuel?"

Manuel glanced up at the guy but didn't wave. "I don't know. I'm so busy, I don't have a chance to talk to my neighbors much."

"This place is remarkable." Earl sounded like an eighth grader on a class field trip. "You always see photos of slums in *National Geographic*, but this is the first time I've experienced the degradation firsthand."

The bicycle-taxi driver took out his keys. "It's like I said, we Cubans are poor."

Manuel's building was much sturdier than many of the shanty-like tar paper and corrugated tin shacks near it. Its cinder block walls looked solid, and Shelby thought it odd the building had no windows. But the thing that really got her attention was its turquoise-colored door with a rusty lock hanging on it. It reminded her of something, but she couldn't quite place what.

Manuel fiddled with the keys. Finally he found what he was looking for and opened the lock. He pushed the door open.

Shelby and Earl were blown away. The walls of Manuel's apartment were iridescent green, and the ceiling was higher than it looked from the outside. The room on one side of the apartment had a table—a four-globe light fixture hanging over it—a chest of drawers and a refrigerator. A filigreed roman arch bisected the apartment, and it wasn't quite apparent what was in the other room except for a lamp with a tan shade and a light switch on the wall.

"You believe this, Shelby?" The poet in Earl's soul was soaring.

Being from Kansas, Shelby couldn't help but share his wonderment. "Yeah, this place is really keen!"

As Shelby calmed down, it came to her where she'd seen the turquoise-colored door with the rusty lock hanging on it. It had been in Hemana's second hut with the Komodo dragons outside! Just then, she heard a mumbling sound. It made her quiver. She took a few steps to look around the roman arch and saw Senator Canfield tied to a chair, a handkerchief gagging his mouth.

Chapter Sixteen

Shelby and Earl heard someone (well, they were figuring it was Manuel but they'd been so preoccupied staring at Senator Canfield) rack the slide of a shotgun. They turned and sure enough, it *was* Manuel.

Shelby was super excited they'd finally found Senator Canfield (it was looking like they wouldn't be de-SEALed and nuclear war could be avoided, after all), but still, she was troubled by why he was bound and gagged in Manuel's apartment, and yeah, also by why Manuel was holding a shotgun on them. "Manuel," she said in a heartfelt way, "this is so unlike you."

Manuel shook his head. "And you Navy SEALs are supposedly America's best warriors?" He laughed scornfully. "Honestly, I don't think either of you idiots could hold down a job slinging burgers."

Shelby bristled because she knew that wasn't true. Her sister Judy slung burgers back in Kansas, and if Judy could handle the job, Shelby surely could too. And really, what did Manuel have to brag about driving a bicycle taxi? "And you're like, a brain surgeon?"

Manuel stuck the shotgun to her forehead. "Maybe not but I could blow your tiny brains out right this second." He seemed to notice the chain and locket around Shelby's neck. He yanked it off.

"Don't!" Shelby lunged for the locket, but with the shotgun stuck to her forehead, she couldn't reach it.

"Ah." Manuel draped the chain around his hand. "Looks like I chanced on something of great value to you."

Shelby was willing to die to get back the locket her parents had given her. But then as she thought about it, that made no sense because if she was dead, she couldn't get the locket back. "No, I don't care. It means nothing to me."

Manuel swung the shotgun off her, tossed the locket onto the floor, and aimed the gun at it. "So you don't care if I blast it to pieces?"

It was brutal biting her tongue, but Shelby remained silent.

Earl nodded. He realized something had been off earlier when Manuel had made the highbrow critiques of his poem. Yes, he surmised that Manuel had probably been *pretending* to be a bicycle-taxi driver. He eyeballed Manuel hard. "I bet you're not really a bicycle-taxi driver."

Manuel laughed and picked up the locket. "Oh my God. Stop it already. You're both killing me. I'm a Russian spy, you idiots! Now rest your feeble brains and pull up a chair next to the politician."

Hearing 'Russian' Shelby instantly thought of her parents being killed by the Russian submarine. But Manuel—a Russian spy? That was crazy. But the more she thought about it, the more she realized it was a possibility. But even if Manuel had been on the sub that killed her parents, it was unlikely that he fired the fatal torpedo. Still, if he was who he said he was, he was a part of the Russian evil empire. Needless to say, Shelby's elation at finding Senator Canfield was fading rapidly. "I hope you realize you're ruining what had been a very happy moment for me, Manuel."

"Oh, I'm so sorry." He gestured with the shotgun. "I said pull up a chair."

"I thought you were a man of high moral integrity," Shelby muttered.

"What was that?" Manuel tracked her with the gun.

"I said I thought you were a man of high moral integrity!"

"Oh, really?" Manuel frowned. "I thought you thought I was a little Cuban eunuch you didn't even want to have sex with."

OOPS-A-NAVY

"Oh, so that's what's *really* bothering you!" Shelby squinted at him.

"Is not."

"Is too!"

Earl interjected, "Shelby, you shouldn't have let him sleep in our tent."

"Oh, get over it, Earl." Earl nursed grudges for*ever!* Maybe she *should've* let the cannibals eat him. "I told you, he didn't do anything."

Manuel said, "She let me use your toothbrush."

That was the final straw, Earl thought. Shelby knew how sensitive he was about his toothbrush! "Is that true, Shelby?"

Shelby rubbed her neck. "Earl, he just told us he's a Russian spy. Are you going to believe him or me?" She felt by phrasing it that way she didn't outright lie. She hoped he would believe her.

Earl slumped his shoulders and his eyes went lifeless. "I've used that toothbrush several times since, and the thought of his germs melding with mine is so worrisome." He turned to Manuel. "You don't have herpes, do you?"

Manuel smiled. "I'm not sure."

"Oh great." Earl shifted from foot to foot, trembling. "I've noticed a little growth on the inside of my cheek."

What a wuss! Shelby thought. All that whining when they ought to be figuring out how they were going to get Senator Canfield out of there and kill Manuel in a particularly brutal way. (The senator looked so uncomfortable, gagged, mumbling, drooling and all. But still, he wore such a pretty robin's egg blue necktie that looked to be silk. Shelby wished she could ask him where he got it. She'd like to buy one for her Uncle Elmer—she never knew what to get him for his birthday.) "Earl, you'll be okay. That bump is just a pimple."

"Are you sure?" He opened his mouth wide for her to look.

She took a quick peek. "Yeah, it's all good in there."

A huge expanse of air eased from Earl's lungs. "Phew. That's a relief."

Manuel held up the shotgun (it seemed the gun was almost as big as him). "What is this, Neurotics Anonymous?" He gestured again with the gun. "I told you once and I'm not telling you again—both of you, pull up chairs alongside the politician."

Shelby grabbed a chair. She knew she should be thinking about escaping and killing Manuel, but she was still wondering about Senator Canfield's tie. "Manuel, did the senator happen to mention where he bought his tie?"

Manuel waved the shotgun. "Nah. It is nice though."

Senator Canfield grunted.

"And you too." Manuel jabbed the shotgun in Earl's direction. "You deaf? Pull up a chair."

Earl was feeling relieved he didn't have herpes, so he was more willing to play ball. "Which chair?"

"I don't care! *Madre de Dios.*" Manuel rolled his eyes.

"Is it okay if I take the one in the corner with the little pillow on it?"

"Yes! Who cares!"

Earl shrugged. "Well, I didn't know. I thought it might be your favorite chair or something."

"It's not my chair!"

Earl nabbed the chair and sat on the other side of Senator Canfield. He tapped elbows with him in what he hoped would be seen as a gesture of solidarity. He knew from reading about the "Hanoi Hilton" during the Vietnam War that communication—no matter how limited—between prisoners was essential for keeping up morale. Earl caught Senator Canfield's eye and winked. When the Senator turned away abruptly (Earl thought he seemed a little disgusted), Earl wondered if he'd gone too far with the wink. Like maybe the senator thought he was gay and coming on to him.

Manuel said, "That's better. Now hands behind your backs."

OOPS-A-NAVY

Earl obeyed. Not that he wanted to necessarily, but Manuel did have a shotgun. Earl was not going to let this experience go to waste though. He was already composing another poem in his head.

Shelby was more hesitant. "Why?"

"Why?" Manuel asked. "Because I want to test your manual dexterity, why else?"

"My manual dexterity is fine. Or maybe you meant my *Manuel* dexterity?" Shelby laughed and folded her hands on her lap.

Manuel fired the shotgun over her head, the buckshot smashing into the wall, raining bits of plaster and dust onto the captives' heads.

Earl brushed the particles off. "I hope there's no asbestos in this stuff. Without a hazmat suit, asbestos can be deadly."

As unlikely as it had first seemed, Shelby was coming to terms with the reality that Manual actually was a Russian spy. She put her hands behind her back.

Manuel hurriedly tied hers and Earl's hands. "Now to shut you up." He pulled a couple of bandannas from a drawer.

"Wait." Shelby searched her mind for how to deal with the situation. "How about if we agree to keep quiet?"

Manuel twirled one of the bandannas into a gag. "I don't think so."

"Wait wait wait." Shelby leaned toward the spy. "What if I was to tell you the latest top-secret Naval intelligence?"

Manuel stopped twirling. "Like what?"

"Like missile silo and Trident nuclear submarine locations around the globe."

Manuel started twirling again. "Yeah, I don't think so."

"Okay, okay." Shelby wasn't out of tricks yet. "What if I could tell you about drug addiction in the highest echelons of the Navy brass?" She was thinking of Bull Gompers overdosing on the magic mushroom smoothie. Which was inadvertent of course, but still, it had happened.

"Ah, I don't know."

"You could release it to WikiLeaks."

Manuel nodded. "Yeah, I could see that maybe. President Putin might dig it. Well, what do you got?"

"Now, Manuel, you know how it works. I give you a little something, you gotta give me a little something back."

Earl burst forth, *"Asbestos poured down like fine snow / A shotgun blast the culprit / The Russian spy had achieved his end / He'd use no bully pulpit."* He looked around expectantly. "And?"

Manuel walked to him, twirling the bandanna. "That makes absolutely no sense."

"Wait, hold on—"

Shelby thought Earl deserved the gagging. Sure, some of his poetry wasn't bad, but he kept forcing it on people, and that last one stunk. *He'd use no bully pulpit.* "Okay." She returned her attention to Manuel. "Now what you can give *me* is to tell me how all this played out. And I think maybe we can get some of that information from the senator himself? As in…" She nodded toward Canfield. "…the gag comes off."

Manuel seemed to need reassurance. "Drug addiction at the highest echelons?"

"The very highest." Which of course wasn't true, Bull being only a rear admiral, two other ranks above hers, but hey, the guy just fired a shotgun over their heads.

Manuel frowned. "Just so you know, the senator hasn't been gagged when I'm around. It's only when I leave that I gotta make sure he doesn't yell. I've been abiding by the Geneva Convention." He removed the senator's gag.

Canfield took a deep breath. "Ah, that's better." He turned to Shelby. "And you are?"

"Navy SEAL Shelby Ryder, Senator, and the captive next to

you is my partner, SEAL Earl Bernstein."

"Well, pleased to meet you," the senator said in his mellifluous radio-quality voice. "And I'm sorry SEAL Bernstein got gagged, but really his poem was so bad."

Earl's heart was breaking. But he knew a poet's life was nothing but suffering. Yes, it hurt, but all was not lost—he would ingest, harvest and conquer this pain to transform it into poetry of immortal genius.

"I guess my first question is for Manuel." Shelby turned to him. "How does a Cuban bicycle-taxi driver, a man of integrity and high morals, end up a Russian spy?"

"First of all, I'm Mexican, not Cuban." Manuel rolled his eyes. "And, Senator, if you want, you can answer this crazy woman's questions, but I can't handle her level of stupidity."

Shelby was quick to respond. "I hear you, Manuel. It's frustrating being around dumb people. And I'll admit it—I'm from Kansas. I promise to be smarter from now on." She was using her Navy SEAL hostage negotiating skills a.k.a. EAT: Empathy Allays Tension.

The senator spoke up. "Shelby, Manuel never was a bicycle-taxi driver."

"I see."

Manuel laughed. "Oh my God, Shelby. Did you really think I just happened to be there every time you needed a ride?"

That's exactly what Shelby had been wondering.

The senator said, "He was casing you, shadowing you and setting you up. Which is exactly how he tricked me. My limo didn't show, and I needed to meet a contact in town. Manuel was there to give me a ride."

"And so, why, Manuel?" Shelby made eye contact. "Why abduct the senator?"

"Why? Because that's what my FSB station chief ordered me to do."

The senator jumped in. "Shelby, the FSB is the successor to the Russian spy agency, the KGB."

All right. Shelby kind of knew that.

"Okay, Shelby," Manuel snarled. "You got what you wanted. Now spill about the drug addiction."

Oh, Shelby really didn't want to give up Bull as a junkie. When WikiLeaks published news of her overdose, it would ruin her career and humiliate the Navy. And it would be bad enough to say Bull was an alcoholic, but if it ever got back to her—saying she'd overdosed on hallucinogenic psilocybin—it would knock her down for the count. Still, a promise was a promise. "It's Bull Gompers."

Manuel stared at Shelby with ill-hidden Russo-Mexican rage. "That's your highest echelon?! I can hardly believe she's still working. That battleaxe should've been put out to pasture twenty years ago. In fact, I'm surprised she's still alive."

Shelby was turning red. "She's a rear admiral, Manuel. That's hardly chopped liver."

Manuel seemed to be calming down. "Well, what about old Bull? Cocaine? Heroin? What did her in?"

Shelby took a deep breath and sighed it out. "She's a magic mushroom addict."

"Ha ha, Shelby." Manuel was not amused. "You mean to tell me an eighty-five-year-old rear admiral is tripping on magic mushrooms? You expect me to believe fairy tales?"

Shelby nodded toward Earl. "If you don't believe me, ask him!"

Manuel seemed to consider her suggestion but passed. "I'm sorry but you and Earl are too stupid to live. I'm going to have to kill you both."

"Oh great." Shelby tried to lay on the guilt. "Here we were talking in good faith. Negotiating. We were empathetic and manifesting goodwill, but now you're like, 'Nope, sorry, end of

OOPS-A-NAVY

good faith. I'm going to have to kill you.' I ask you, is that fair?"

"Perfectly fair," Manuel said, but his guilty tone gave away that he was at least a little disturbed by the ethical implications.

Shelby sat up on the chair. "And so you're just going to shotgun all three of us right here in this run-down, crappy apartment?"

Manuel's brow furrowed. "I thought you liked my apartment. You were raving about it before."

Shelby scowled. "I was flattering you because you're this little four-foot-nine Cuban bicycle-taxi driver with no life."

"I told you I'm Mexican! And I'm five-one!"

"Doesn't matter." Shelby spat. "This place is a pit and you're pitiful."

Earl chewed through his gag. "Oooh, Shelby, that's got artistic panache—pit and pitiful."

Manuel shrugged. "Doesn't matter, Shelby. I know in my heart you liked it. And, yeah, you have to die."

"So is it true…" Earl was excited to be a part of the conversation again. "…you're going to shotgun all three of us?"

Manuel squared his shoulders and looked Earl in the eye. "No."

"Oh, thank God," Earl said. "For a minute, I really thought you were going to, and if you had, my mother would've never forgiven me for not becoming a proctologist."

Without missing a beat, Manuel continued, "I'm only killing you and Shelby. I need to keep the senator alive until after the election, and then I'm releasing him because killing him would cause a nuclear war. And Vlad's not up for that just yet."

"Shotgunned to death." Earl's bottom lip quivered. "What a way to go." Then he considered things. "But ultimately there are worse ways to die. You could fall into a volcano. You could be tied to a stake and eaten by jackals. You could be trapped in a porta-potty in the North Pole and freeze to death."

"And there were the cannibals," Shelby chipped in. "That would hardly have been a peaceful death."

Earl nodded. "Right."

Manuel shook his head. "What's with you two? Are you taking stupid pills or what?"

"I think there's something you need to understand about these two, Manuel," the senator said gravely. "They're not afraid of death."

"Oh, no?" Manuel scoffed.

The senator sat up in his chair, a gleam in his eye. "They're United States Navy SEALs, America's elite fighting force. They can swim underwater with machine guns, that somehow work after that. They can fall from the sky (well, parachute) and land on their feet, not tumbling like ordinary parachuters. They ride Killer Whales (like they used to at Sea World before the Killer Whales started killing the riders). Members of the opposite sex swoon in their presence. (Which is why most of the guys sign up to be SEALs in the first place.) Romance writers make their livings writing about them. They were born of the water and live on the water."

Manuel had heard enough. "And they'll die on the water, Senator. In fact, tomorrow morning at six. And ironically on a fishing boat called *The Real Seal*. Write a poem about *that*, Earl!"

Chapter Seventeen

The next morning came around too fast. Sure enough, one thing Manuel said had come true—Earl had converted the terrifying news of Shelby's and his impending demise into a poem. And even as Manuel bicycled them down the hill from his apartment (and it was a lot easier going down the hill than coming up), Earl was determined to practice his craft.

He cleared his throat. "Okay, here goes. *Their death would be in water / Fitting, for their life gave no quarter / As SEALs lie in the sun, their skins browned / Now as SEALs still, they would be drowned.*"

Despite the stressful situation and as tired as she was of Earl's poetry, Shelby had to admit this last one was pretty good. "That's really not bad, Earl."

"Aww, Shelby." He leaned over and kissed her cheek. "You'll never know how much you saying that means to me."

Manuel rolled his eyes. "Trust me, it wasn't that good."

"Manuel." The wind—created from going downhill—in her face, Shelby thought they were rolling awfully fast. A marketplace, huge skids of bananas, avocados and papayas under a blue- and white-striped awning, seemed to fly by. "Aren't we going too fast?!"

"Yeah." The little Mexican-turned-Russian spy was sweating. "The extra weight is adding to our momentum. I've never had passengers going down this hill before."

"But don't you have brakes?"

"Nah, I never needed them before. Hang on!"

Somehow they made it to the bottom of the hill in one piece, but they were still flying.

Then Earl had an idea. "Shelby, since we're going to die,

think we could do some more kissing? We don't have to do tongue—but that would be nice."

"Oh, Earl, I don't think so." Shelby was panting from the roller coaster-like ride down the hill. "That way I would go into the hereafter feeling like a total loser."

"Nice try, Earl." Manuel wiped the sweat from his brow.

Shelby could smell the sea's salty air. The ocean was at hand. And her thoughts went black. She thought of how she hadn't avenged her parents' deaths. (And Manuel still had the precious locket they'd given her!) She thought about how she hadn't accomplished anything at all really.

They pulled into the dock area, which was shaped like a big L, royal palm trees standing ramrod straight, their fronds flicking in the breeze. Cigarette boats sat Miami Vice-like in a row along the dock. They were powerful boats with sleek fiberglass bodies and triple-outboard motors. Shelby read their names as Manuel slowed his pedaling. *Oceanrunner. Nitro. Mad Max. Pocket Rocket.* Finally, they came to what looked like a crappy Vietnamese fishing boat. It sat away from the cigarette boats, tied at the end of a little pier, shunned like a redheaded stepchild.

This can't be our boat, Shelby thought. It was the anti-powerboat. Not a cigarette boat, but a cigarette-butt boat. Maybe twenty-five feet long, sitting low in the water like a one-foot wave could swamp it, the boat had a sun-faded red canopy over its midsection and two squat, blue plastic half-barrels in back. The boat's dirty white paint was peeling, and at the waterline the wood rotting. Oddly, it had an inboard motor, which meant it had probably been decent back in the day, but now it hardly looked seaworthy. The boat drifted sideways in a departing cigarette boat's wake, and sure enough, in fading, flaking, algae-stained scum between the boat's two exhausts read: *The Real Seal.*

Shelby was indignant. "If you're going to kill us, you ought to at least do it on a decent boat."

OOPS-A-NAVY

Manuel smirked as he—checking to see no one was looking—herded them onto the boat. "You can sit here." He shoved Shelby down onto one of the barrels, where she found herself stuck like a ladybug on its back in a thimbleful of super glue. Manuel eyed the other barrel and turned to Earl. "Your turn."

"Sorry, Manuel." Earl was straightforward with him. "I can't sit there. I get pain in my sciatic nerve whenever I'm in that position. You can ask Shelby."

"He does, Manuel. Whenever he goes to the dentist, he experiences excruciating nerve pain when they lean him back in the chair. I've heard his cries."

"Nice try, bozos." Manuel pushed Earl down onto the barrel. "All right." He headed for the boat's bridge under the canopy.

Shelby heard the inboard motor gurgle to life. It was a sound someone didn't normally hear in Kansas. A unique sound really. Like if you're from Ecuador, and it's the first time you hear a furnace kick in on a snowy night. She wished they didn't have their hands tied behind their backs, though—this would be a good time to escape.

Earl was waxing poetic. They could tie his hands but not his mind. "Here's my latest. *Into the barrel he goes / When to come out no one knows / For sure it will pain his sciatic nerve / Seems like life threw him a curve.*" He looked over at Shelby. "What do you think?"

She thought he was a lunatic for composing a poem when he should be thinking about escaping. But hey, they were going to die soon, so what was the point of dissing him? "It's brilliant, Earl. You're a very stable genius."

"You're not just saying that?" Earl had a tear in his eye.

"Well." But really, she didn't want to hear any more poems. What if Manuel took them on a long boat ride before killing them? She wouldn't be able to handle hearing any more. "No, Earl, of course I wasn't just saying that. But really I'd make that your last poem, your crowning achievement."

"But what if new inspiration hits? I may be able to add to my body of work."

Manuel returned from the bridge. "You recite any more of your poems, I'll set a giant hook in you and troll you as shark bait."

Shelby wondered how that would work. The sharks would really just tear at him here and there. It would be very unlikely they would chomp down directly on the hook. So in that sense Earl wouldn't be effective bait. But nah, Manuel was just trying to scare Earl into silence. Typical Russian censorship. And that was just plain wrong. But still, she was glad Manuel was doing it because she couldn't stand to hear another one of Earl's poems either. But she couldn't tell Earl that. She said, "It's somewhere in the US Constitution, Earl. Free speech is your right."

Earl suddenly looked encouraged. "Yeah! That's right!"

Shelby laughed. "Was that a pun?"

"Idiots!" Manuel threw up his hands and went back to the bridge.

Earl felt the boat surge forward. They were off on their last journey. And no, he wouldn't let Manuel's threats stop him from being artistic. At least they were on a slow boat. It would give him more time to be creative before the dreaded end came. And really, being wedged in the barrel wasn't that bad. Yes, he felt little electrical impulses in his sciatic nerve, but the pain was quite manageable.

Shelby had time to think too. She didn't mind the barrel either. It was kind of like being in a recliner. And seagulls were flying out into the open sea along with them. It was really quite beautiful. But then she realized the only reason the birds were accompanying them was because they anticipated a meal. Like when Earl and Shelby would get thrown overboard. That dampened her enthusiasm for them. Even worse, Manuel still had the locket her dearly missed parents had given her. That hurt the most.

"How we doing back there?" Manuel called as if they were on a family outing.

The irony scathed Earl's soul. He was on the verge of learned helplessness.

Shelby would try the reverse psychology she'd learned in a Navy SEAL course about being held captive in impossible situations. "Actually, Manuel, I'm happy you're doing this."

Earl looked at her, deeply hurt and not a little confused. "How can you say that, Shelby?"

Shelby shook her head and said softly so Manuel couldn't overhear, "Don't you remember Ms. Suharto's class 'Jujitsu of the mind: killing the enemy mentally before they kill you'?"

Earl tapped his teeth together twice. "I don't think I took that one. Was that a requirement?"

"Nah, it was an elective, but I got a lot out of it. I really think they should make it a requirement."

Manuel called, "What are you two psychos babbling about back there?"

Shelby said, "About how grateful we are for you."

Earl winked at her. "Yeah, Manuel. You're the best."

"Why, thanks, guys. You're making this a lot easier for me."

Earl sighed. It didn't look like the mental jujitsu was working all that great. And the sun was starting to get to him. He was fair skinned, and it didn't take long for him to burn. "Manuel, I'm going to need sunscreen."

"Oh, Earl," Shelby muttered. She felt she'd been making inroads with Manuel with the reverse psychology, and now Earl might blow it.

"Ah hell, why not?" Manuel stuck a stick in the steering wheel to keep the boat on course for the open sea and pulled out a drawer in the bridge. He removed a tube of sunscreen and read the label. "Is 30 SPF okay?"

Earl raised his eyebrows. "You don't have 50?"

"No, that's all I've got."

"Okay, I guess that'll have to do."

Huh. Shelby thought maybe they might be getting somewhere with Manuel after all. "That's very nice of you, Manuel. Earl burns easily."

Earl spontaneously rhapsodized a poem, "*Manuel, Manuel, our friend for life / Manuel, Manuel, he's done with strife / Sunscreen he brings to stop a burn / He's always the man, well, to do a good turn.*" Earl couldn't help but laugh appreciatively at the genius of that last "man, well" pun on Manuel's name.

Shelby was deathly sick of his poetry. Oh God. But here came Manuel with the sunscreen.

Manuel opened the cap on the tube. "Here you go."

Earl bit his lip. "Is it within the expiration date?"

"Huh?" Manuel examined the tube. "I don't know. It doesn't say anything. I think it's okay."

"Well." Earl squinted at him. "Were you just going to use it on me without being sure? You know old sunscreen only *increases* the potential for a burn *and* it causes breast enlargement in males."

"Well, I was thinking it's better than nothing." Manuel sounded hurt. "You know, every time I try to do something nice for you two, you pull some stunt like this, or say one of your lousy poems."

"Wait a minute." Shelby had an idea. "I remember running into this before. Just look at the bottom of the tube. There should be a number."

Manuel checked. "Yeah, there's a number, but it's not a date."

"Well, the first two numbers will be the year it was manufactured and the last three will be the day. And the sunscreen will be good for three years from that date."

OOPS-A-NAVY

Manuel seemed to be doing the mental figuring. He laughed. "What do you know! It's still good for another four months!"

"Cool." Shelby saw this as serious reverse psychology progress. "Now you're going to untie him so he can apply it, right?"

"Oh." Manuel hesitated. "Can't I put it on him? He doesn't have any skin diseases I need to worry about, does he?"

Shelby's eyes lit up. "Oh, yeah. He's got a case of that flesh-eating bacteria."

Earl frowned. "What are you talking about, Shelby? I don't have that. I get a little eczema when I get really upset sometimes but that's not contagious."

Manuel put his hands on his hips. "You sure it's not?"

"Positive, Manuel." Earl nodded. "You can apply the sunscreen worry-free, and besides, it would be really hard for me to apply it to my face without a mirror anyway."

Shelby rolled her eyes. A golden opportunity gone! She resolved that if Manuel didn't kill Earl she would.

Manuel was applying the sunscreen.

"Just get my nose good." Earl seemed to be enjoying the attention. "That burns the quickest. That and the tips of my ears."

"I already got your ears." Manuel looked out to the front of the boat. An aircraft carrier approached rapidly. "Holy crap!" He ran to the bridge, removed the stick holding the wheel in place and spun the wheel.

In the sudden turn, both barrels, and Earl and Shelby in them, tipped.

"Hey!" Earl cried. "I think some of the sunscreen on my nose got rubbed off. Manuel, you'll have to reapply."

Meanwhile, Manuel waved to the giant gray powerhouse of a ship, ten stories above them, as it narrowly missed *The Real Seal*, sending the boat away from it on its wake, like an outrigger canoe riding a wave.

Shelby looked up just in time to see the carrier. She knew the ship's 50-caliber guns could cut *The Real Seal* to ribbons in a flash. Only thing was, that was undesirable since they were on it. Still, Shelby couldn't help but yell. "Help! We're Navy SEALs trapped by a Russian spy of Mexican descent! Help!"

The sailors obviously didn't hear, because they just stood on the boat's deck waving their white caps. True, a few of them seemed to be wondering why two of the people on the crappy little boat were lying on the floor with their hands tied behind their backs, but they just kept waving anyway.

"Shelby!" Manuel was mortified. "Quit yelling!" He kept smiling and waving to the sailors but continued talking to Shelby. "We were getting along so nicely. I put the sunscreen on Earl. And now you're betraying me!"

Well, that was ironic, Shelby thought. *We're* betraying *him*? She took one last look and saw the aircraft carrier drifting out of range. "Ha ha, that's funny, Manuel. I gave you Jalapeño SPAM. I let you stay in our tent and massage my naked feet. I let you use Earl's toothbrush—"

"That was so wrong, Shelby." Earl shot her a glare.

"—and you say we betrayed *you*!" Shelby was discouraged, sure. By Manuel. But also by missing out on the sailors. For certainly the sailors would've helped them had they known they were Navy SEALs. But she fortified herself with the fact that Navy SEALs *never* give up. Well, she thought, hardly ever anyway. "Can you at least set us up in the barrels again? It's really awkward down here on the floor. It's wet and smells fishy. Really, you shouldn't have put us in plastic barrels with no weight in the bottom in the first place. They were a tipping hazard from the get-go."

Earl piped up saying, "And you may as well figure on reapplying the sunscreen everywhere. I clearly felt it get rubbed off my nose, but it may have come off other places too."

OOPS-A-NAVY

Manuel spat. "I'll set you up, Shelby. And I'll make sure I put plenty of weight in the barrels too so there won't be a tipping hazard. Earl, yeah, no problem. I'll reapply everywhere." He set the barrels back up. "Now, there are actually little ledges in the barrels so when I get you in, you can sit."

"Why the hell didn't you tell us that before?" Shelby was thinking that was such a careless oversight.

Manuel shrugged. "Well, I was in kind of a hurry—there were people on the docks—and I didn't think of it, okay? You know, you guys can be so demanding. I have to think of everything. Okay, ladies first." He picked up Shelby and helped her climb into the barrel.

Shelby wasn't fooled by his sudden gallantry. But it *was* more comfortable sitting on the ledge.

"And now Earl." He did the same for Earl.

"Uh, the sunscreen?"

"Real soon, Earl. Real soon. First I want to stabilize the barrels so there will be no more tipping accidents." He disappeared into the boat's galley and returned with a big sack.

"What's that?" Shelby was getting suspicious of the little Mexican-turned-Russian spy.

"A bag of sand." He smiled at Shelby. "It'll keep you from tipping. Or in your Navy lingo, just think of it as ballast." He started pouring the sand into Earl's barrel.

Shelby craned her neck to look. "That doesn't look like sand to me, buster!"

"Who's Buster?" Earl was confused. "It's just me, you, and Manuel."

Shelby frowned. "It's just an expression we use in Kansas. Like 'bud' or 'jack.' Do I have to explain everything to you?"

"You don't have to get testy."

Shelby turned her attention back to Manuel. "That looks more like pulverized limestone than sand to me."

Manuel blushed. "Nah, it's just white sand."

"Well, I guess that's possible, but it looks too clumpy for sand."

"Trust me." He finished filling Earl's barrel and now filled Shelby's.

"Trust *you*? Ha ha. That's a laugh." Shelby knew saying that could be counterproductive for the reverse-psychology atmosphere she'd been trying to cultivate, but she couldn't help herself.

Manuel disappeared into the galley again and this time returned with a big bucket of water. He dumped several gallons into Earl's barrel.

"Hey, what's that for?" Earl stared with wide eyes. "And I'm still waiting on the sunscreen. I feel like I'm frying."

Manuel explained, "The water will keep you cool. That white sand can get so hot. Haven't you ever been on a beach too hot to walk on? You know, you have to go back to your motel room to get sandals?"

Earl didn't flinch. "A beach hasn't been made that's too hot for a Navy SEAL to walk on."

Finally, Shelby thought. The SEAL in Earl was kicking in. But, as Manuel poured gallons of water into her barrel, she doubted his explanation of needing the water because the sand became too hot. Now, Manuel had a big stick and was stirring inside Earl's barrel. Then it hit Shelby! If it *was* pulverized limestone, not sand, pulverized limestone mixed with water made —cement!

"What the heck is going on here, Manuel?!" Shelby cried. She tried to move her legs. She felt like a giant mouse stuck in a glue trap. Still, she managed to muscle one leg out. "Earl, it's cement! Climb out!"

"Hey, Shelby!" Manuel was taking no guff. "Get your leg back in there! You're creating another tipping hazard!"

OOPS-A-NAVY

"I don't think so, Manuel. What *I* think is that you're up to no good."

Manuel shook his head. "You shouldn't be judging people like that, Shelby. Tell you what. Climb back in and I'll untie your hands."

"Mine too?" Earl seemed excited.

"Yours too."

Shelby figured the proposed tradeoff meant something was up. She smelled a rat. Not that she actually smelled a rat, or knew what a rat smelled like. Like 'buster' or 'jack' it was just another expression.

Earl remembered a tip from a hostage negotiation class he'd taken during Hell Week—when the hostage taker gets involved in a give and take exchange with the hostages, it's an excellent sign. "I think we should accept his offer, Shelby." And Earl couldn't move his legs at this point, so he figured he might as well get something out of the deal.

"Well, okay." Shelby nodded toward Earl. "Then go ahead, commie, untie him."

Manuel was stern. "Put your leg back in first."

But Shelby was steadfast, immovable (well, psychologically, not because of the cement. Although she was that too, at least one leg was). "No. Earl gets untied first."

Manuel spat again but he untied Earl. He turned to Shelby. "There. Now put your leg back in."

"Now untie *me*." Shelby was done being fooled by his trickery.

"That's not fair." Manuel's nostrils flared. "You said so yourself—when one side gives a little, the other has to as well. I gave you something. Now you gotta give me something back."

Shelby shook her head. "All true, but you gave Earl something. Not me."

"Unfair."

"Those are the facts. Now are you going to untie me or not, Montel?"

"It's Manuel."

"Manuel, Montel, Tommy James and the Shondells. I don't care what your name is. Are you going to untie me?"

The little Mexican stomped his foot but untied her. "Oh, your wrists are really red. Do you want some lotion?"

Shelby examined her wrists. "What do you have?"

"I think it's called Retro Care. I always keep a bottle onboard in case my hands get dry."

Shelby was hating him less and less, and yet, she reminded herself that ultimately, he was up to no good. "Yeah, okay, I'll try it and see if it helps."

He went down into the galley.

Earl made use of his absence. "Shelby, I don't think he's going to give me more sunscreen."

"Oh, Earl, I wouldn't worry about it. You don't look burnt to me."

"Thanks, but you know how you always look okay in the sun, but then when you get in the shower you're red as a bald eagle's egg?"

"Are bald eagle's eggs red? I never knew that."

Manuel was back. "I found the lotion, but it's just Target's generic version."

Earl wasted no time. "What about my sunscreen?"

"Oh." Manuel grimaced. "I just used the last of it, Earl. Sorry." He gave Shelby the lotion.

"Thanks."

"Hey, what am I doing?" Manuel slapped his forehead as if a mosquito was injecting the deadly Zika virus into his brain. "Okay, I untied you, so you gotta put your leg back in the barrel. Right now!"

Shelby, figuring a deal was a deal, gave it a try. "Sorry,

OOPS-A-NAVY

Manuel, but the cement has already set."

"Damn it, Shelby! You should've put it in as soon as we made the deal."

"Well, you should've stuck to your guns and made me."

"She's right, Manuel." Earl rubbed his wrists. "She's right on this one."

"Oh, shut up." Manuel picked up a gaff that had been lying on the floor and waved it around wildly. "I've had it with both of you. You're going over!"

And just like that Earl and Shelby realized why they'd been cast in cement—even though they were SEALs and expert swimmers, they wouldn't be able to swim with two hundred pounds of cement attached to them. No way.

"This is dastardly." Shelby scowled at the wee Mexican.

"Well, you knew I had to kill you. And I'm not getting sucked into any more of your reverse-psychology ploys either."

"Yes." Shelby tried to lay on the guilt. "But to kill a SEAL by drowning is disrespectful."

"Well, how should I have killed you?"

Earl interjected, "Any way but drowning."

"Exactly," Shelby confirmed. "Do you have a gun? You can shoot us."

"I left the shotgun in my apartment."

Shelby shrugged. "Well, take us back to your apartment and shoot us."

"But I was really hoping to get this over with. And now, with you in the barrels with the cement…" He shook his head. "…it would be too hard getting you back there. No, sorry, you're going over."

Shelby motioned with her free leg. "Hack us to death with the gaff, then."

Earl winced. "I don't know about that, Shelby. I think I'd rather go over."

"Look!" Manuel's face flushed red. "You don't get to choose how you're going to die." He motioned to the wide-open rollicking sea. "Over you go, both of you."

"Well." Shelby was suddenly so emotional. "Can I at least have my locket back?"

Manuel straightened his shoulders. "Sorry."

"Why not?"

"Why not? Because it's valuable. I should be able to get at least a hundred bucks for it, and what are you…" He looked out at the deep, bottomless ocean. "…going to do with it down there?"

"Fine."

"Okay, I don't have all day." Manuel clapped his hands twice. He stepped toward them. "Chop-chop. Over you go."

Earl hesitated. "One final request? Can we go over holding hands?"

"Oh, you know, for Navy SEALs you two really are wimpy." He bit his lip. "But what the hell. Okay."

"Decent of you," Earl offered.

Shelby wasn't quite as pleased with the concession, but at least it was something. Her original take on Manuel had been right—he was a man of high morals and integrity. Well, at least a little anyway. "Yes. We appreciate it."

"Okay, then. I can't swim, so the boat being so low with all this extra weight is making me really nervous. Of course once you go over, the boat will level off and I'll be able to relax." Manuel pushed them all the way to the very back edge of the boat, which was really low in the water now. "All right, no big speeches. You can see how the boat is dangerously listing, so just hold hands and over you go."

Earl had a tear in his eye again. "One final request?"

"You already made one final request. No, I'm sorry. No."

"Okay then, a final final request?" Earl was visibly angry, his ears turning red. Although, granted, some of that color may have

OOPS-A-NAVY

been from sunburn.

Manuel sighed. "What is it?"

"My last poem."

"Oh my God." Manuel sat on the side of the boat and put his fingertips to his temples. "I'm sorry, Earl, but I can't allow that."

"Why not?"

"Because it's really not fair to Shelby and me."

Shelby wiped the tear from Earl's eye. "Oh, Manuel, for old time's sake, let him."

Manuel threw up his hands. "Okay. Whatever you say. But this is it. No more final or final final or final final final requests."

Earl took a deep breath and held Shelby's hand. *"Shelby, Shelby, first female divine / I would never hang you out on a vine / Troubles we've had and troubles we've met / We didn't choose each other but you get what you get / So Fate has cordoned us off together / To endure both sunny skies and stormy weather—"*

"Earl." Manuel was twirling the ends of his mustache. "How much longer? And that stormy weather line was really cliché."

"Just one more verse." Earl caught Shelby's eye. *"So Shelby, my partner, I didn't much like you at the start / And still don't like you when you insult my art / But you showed yourself true to the Navy blue / And made me proud to serve with you."*

Manuel picked up the gaff. "All right, that was actually two verses, but okay, over you go."

Shelby squeezed Earl's hand. "That was beautiful."

"Really?"

"Let's go!" Manuel approached with the gaff.

No, not really, Shelby was thinking. It had just been something nice to say. But now that he was pressing her, she didn't want to lie. But still, they would be dead soon…

Manuel pushed them off with the gaff.

Chapter Eighteen

Well, being SEALs, Shelby and Earl were used to being in the water, but this was substantially different. No, this time they were in big trouble. They just hoped not to get chomped by sharks, which were notorious for hitting vulnerable prey, before they drowned.

But before long, they were caught up in a mesh net. They didn't have their diving masks, so it was difficult to see, but they noticed a blurry light moving around underwater. It could be an angel, Shelby thought. Or perhaps even the presence of God. But it was more likely a flashlight, one that could work underwater though, because not all flashlights can, and it was definitely getting closer.

Earl recognized her first. He turned to Shelby. He wanted to say, "Holy crap, Shelby, it's Bull Gompers!" but being underwater he was unable to. But he pointed excitedly to the octogenarian rear admiral.

Sure enough, Bull Gompers came swimming up to them in full frogman gear, diving mask, scuba tank, flippers, an RPG over her shoulder, and she was holding what looked to be a helium tank that could be blasted into a flaccid weather balloon. Bull buddy-breathed with them a couple of times and then pointed up at the surface as if asking for their permission to go along with her plan.

Earl and Shelby, true to their SEAL roots—and of course they were drowning—were game, giving her enthusiastic thumbs-up signs.

Bull seemed relieved. She jammed the helium tank into the opening of the weather balloon and triggered an explosive charge that shot buoyant gas into the balloon, which filled like a balloon inflated by a carnival guy who then twists it into a funny hat, like a dachshund, but this balloon wasn't getting twisted and was a lot bigger.

Bull put Shelby's and Earl's hands on the handles at the base of the balloon, and soon enough the balloon began to rise, dragging them all upward. Sure, they were still vulnerable to sharks, but the sharks may have been baffled by the huge balloon. They might've thought it was a giant octopus that expelled an even more gigantic fart, catapulting it upward.

The balloon burst through the ocean surface and into the bright Caribbean sunshine.

Shelby and Earl gasped for air! They were astonished that they'd been saved! Especially that they'd been saved by Bull Gompers. Not that they would've thought Bull wouldn't save them. She was a SEAL after all and SEALs did that sort of thing for each other, but the last they knew of her she'd been a magic mushroom addict, lusting for Hemana, and Dr. Cooke had knocked her out with a powerful sedative that left her near death. So yeah, they were surprised by her saving them, and they were also surprised by *how* they'd been saved. They definitely hadn't envisioned getting saved by a giant weather balloon. They wiped their eyes as the balloon carried them higher into the air, and then they saw Manuel piloting *The Real Seal* back to port. In the distance the aircraft carrier loomed immense. It looked like it was barely moving.

They continued to rise, now being able to take in the island itself. And the higher they got, the colder the air became. Much colder.

Now Bull was preparing the RPG. She was aiming it at *The Real Seal*! Neither Shelby nor Earl were sad about that. They were just surprised Bull had an RPG in the first place. Then it hit Shelby! If Bull sank *The Real Seal*, she'd never get back the locket her parents had given her. It would go down with Manuel and the boat!

Shelby knew how stubborn Bull was about disrupting her plans, but she had to try. "Admiral, please don't shoot!"

Bull took her eye from the RPG. "Why the hell not? That's the little Mexican-turned-commie who kidnapped you and is holding Senator Canfield hostage."

"Wow." Earl raised an eyebrow. Bull had great intel.

"All true, ma'am, but the little commie has the locket my dead parents gave me, and if you sink the boat, I'll never see it again."

"Ryder." Bull rested the RPG on her shoulder. "How could your dead parents give you anything?"

"Oh, I just said that wrong. They were actually alive when they gave it to me."

Bull racked the RPG. "Sorry, Ryder. Collateral damage."

"It means the world to her, Admiral," Earl intervened.

Shelby was touched by Earl's support. She was glad she hadn't told him his final poem was crappy, and glad he hadn't died from the poison-drug blow dart. Well, pretty much glad anyway.

Bull frowned but eased down the RPG. "You two owe me for this—I really wanted to blast the little red."

Earl's arms were getting tired from hanging onto the balloon handles with the two hundred pounds of cement attached to his legs, and he was thoroughly convinced the salt water had removed all his sunscreen and now, especially in the higher altitudes, he was getting a third-degree sunburn. Worse yet, he was cold, shivering. Still, what Bull had said threw him. "Why do *I* owe you?"

"Just because you're you, Bernstein. 'Nuff said."

Earl thought that was particularly mean-spirited, but Bull *had* saved them, so he was willing to let it go.

"Thanks, Admiral." Shelby was truly grateful. Sure, she still didn't have the locket, but at least now there was a chance of recovering it. And, like Earl, she was noticing that with the two hundred pounds of added weight, her arms were getting tired, and she too was freezing. Yes, they'd done drills like this with no safety lines—hanging from helicopters with two hundred-pound weights strapped to them—but still, she wasn't going to be able to hang on forever. "Uh, Admiral, how are we getting back to land? It's getting hard to hang on and so cold."

"Ryder, have you forgotten that you're a SEAL?"

Shelby wasn't surprised by that comeback. "But even so, we need to get to land or we're going to freeze to death. What's your plan?"

"Well." Bull wriggled out of her scuba tank harness and let the tank drop. The tank fell for a very long time before hitting the green-blue water with the tiniest of splashes, and when it did, they realized they were *a lot* higher than they'd thought. "I knew that the aircraft carrier was going to be at roughly the same coordinates as your stinky little boat and I'd *meant*..." She frowned. "...to bring along a flare gun."

"You forgot a flare gun!" Earl was discouraged beyond belief. And now he was really shivering. From his Surviving in Extremely High Altitude (SEHA) course during Hell Week, he knew it would only be moments before they entered "the death zone," where a person lost consciousness, and he wondered, quite frankly, if that was already starting to happen to Bull.

"Hey, Einstein!"

Bull always called Earl that when she got excited, Shelby thought. "It's Bernstein, Admiral."

"Whatever-stein!" Bull cuffed Earl's ear. "If you were eighty-five and coming off of a magic mushroom overdose, I'd like to see if you'd remember!"

Earl rubbed his ear but thought she kind of had a point.

Shelby, always the cool head, said, "Admiral, you're still

feeling the effects of the overdose?"

"Ah, hell, Ryder, it's no worse than hangovers I've had after drinking a host of Marines under the table."

"Well, ma'am." Earl tried to maintain an even strain, but he could feel his extremities beginning to freeze and his strength giving out. "I think it's great you saved us, but now we're headed for the death zone."

Bull sighed. "Yeah, I knew that could be a problem."

Shelby asked, "So what are we going to do?"

Bull smiled. "I say we put our heads together."

It wasn't easy but they managed to put their heads together, Earl's head even conking Bull's. Earl didn't think he hurt her and was disappointed he didn't. After a while, they put their heads back apart.

Bull looked at them. "Well, that didn't accomplish anything."

Shelby gripped the balloon handles even tighter. "Actually, I think we were supposed to think too."

"So it's all over?" Earl could feel his lungs filling with tiny ice crystals. At least that's how it felt. (He didn't know if that's what actually happened in the death zone but it seemed plausible.)

"Meh," Bull said, gung-ho to the last. "We still might get out of this."

Shelby stared at her. More specifically at the RPG slung over her shoulder. "Hey, what about the RPG?"

Bull glanced at it. "You didn't want me to shoot the little commie."

Shelby rolled her eyes. "No, I mean, couldn't shooting it function as a flare gun? Like an SOS?"

Earl laughed. "Shelby, that's the dumbest idea I ever heard. You're talking about shooting a live grenade."

"Why…" Bull's eyes lit up. "…I bet it could, Ryder!" She unslung the RPG. "I'll just shoot it across the aircraft carrier's bow and they're bound to see who fired it." She chipped ice off the huge gun's trigger mechanism.

"You sure you're up to this, Admiral?" That was Shelby's way of asking if Bull wanted her to fire the powerful gun for her.

"Hell yeah, Ryder. I used to practice with these on the range all the time. Blowing up old tanks, abandoned autos, refrigerators. It was a blast!"

"All right, then." Shelby still wasn't sure about it, but they had to try something soon.

Bull hefted the huge rocket-propelled grenade launcher onto her shoulder. She leaned her eye down to the optical sight. "Now if I figure right, this should go directly over the top of the carrier's observation deck. They won't be able to miss it!"

"Go for it, Admiral!" Earl said. He was surprised the words even came out as he was quite sure he had ice in his trachea. And he wondered if he was getting burned *worse* through the thin layer of ice now coating his entire body. But he told himself to pay attention to Bull's big shot. This was important.

Bull pulled the trigger and a fiery flash shot from the back of the gun, and the kickback sent her legs flying. Like a flag stretched out in a hurricane, Shelby thought, or actually it would be a cyclone if they'd been in the Southern Hemisphere or a typhoon in the Eastern. She had no idea why the storm had so many names. She got to thinking, what happened if a hurricane crossed from the Southern to the Northern Hemisphere? Would it turn into a cyclone? So much in life was confusing. But she returned her attention to what was happening. This was important.

Bull's legs swung back now, and she inadvertently kicked Earl in the balls. Hard.

"Oh God, that hurt!" Even though Earl's body was frozen, and he wouldn't have thought he could feel that much pain—he did.

"Sorry, Einstein." Bull looked at him semi-compassionately. "Good thing I wasn't wearing my pointy-toe stilettos though."

They all turned to watch the grenade as it sizzled across the luscious blue Caribbean sky. This was important.

"It's looking good," Shelby avowed. Her arms were so tired and frigid, but somehow she managed to cross her fingers for luck.

Bull adjusted her glasses. She mumbled, "Hail Mary, full of grace…"

The grenade didn't quite make it over the observation deck. It slammed into an F-16 fighter jet on the flight deck, exploding it in a fireball.

They were all disappointed and not a little concerned as to what this might mean for them. But the good news was that all kinds of firefighters scrambled onto the flight deck and were pointing up at the weather balloon.

"Hallelujah! We've been sighted!" Bull cried.

Shelby sighed, so relieved to have yet again been saved from the brink of death.

Earl was in too much pain to think much of anything.

But wait! The aircraft carrier's massive 50-caliber guns were swiveling toward the weather balloon.

"What the hell." Bull's mouth dropped open.

The guns burst forth in a blaze of orange fiery death, peppering the sky with anti-aircraft flak. The three of them could see it coming.

"No, we're friendlies!" Shelby yelled. She would have waved her arms, too, but to wave her arms she would have had to let go of the weather balloon, and she would have fallen into the ocean, so, less effective than waving her arms as it might be, she settled for continued yelling.

Bull gritted her teeth. "I know the commanding officer on that carrier and believe you me, he's going to hear about this outrage." Then she seemed to think about it. "Of course, at the same time, I can understand why he's unhappy."

OOPS-A-NAVY

Earl finally managed to make a sound. He said, "Ow."

The good news was the flak punctured the weather balloon, and so they were descending, their iced bodies defrosting as they did. The bad news was the flak kept hitting the balloon, and they were descending much faster than was safe. In fact—they were plummeting.

Bull shrugged and looked at Shelby and Earl. "Any ideas?"

Shelby thought the only real chance would be if they happened to land in Manuel's boat. But even if they managed that, with the weight of the cement in the half-barrels they would crash through the floor and sink anyway. On top of everything else, Manuel and *The Real Seal* were long gone.

Shelby had dropped into the sea from helicopters at a thousand feet in Navy SEAL training exercises, so she had an idea of what to do and she shouted instructions. "Land feet first! Elbows in tight, one hand covering your nose and mouth and the other hand holding that hand at the wrist!"

Bull tucked in her elbows.

Earl just figured his balls were going to get ripped off.

Bull was humming "Anchors Away" when they hit.

Fortunately, the cement barrels broke most of Shelby's and Earl's fall (Earl was relieved his balls weren't ripped off), and Bull was so light she managed to avoid injury altogether, but she lost her glasses, which were old—she'd gotten more than her fair share of use out of them—but still, they were her favorite pair. Fortunately, the balloon was keeping them afloat in the water for now, but unfortunately, sharks started circling (although Bull couldn't see them without her glasses), and if the sharks didn't rip them to shreds, as the balloon continued deflating, they'd soon sink and drown.

Just then a motorboat came by pulling a skier. The skier, a woman, maybe seventy, in just a bikini bottom and with a tattoo of a motorcycle on her lower back, was slumped so far forward hanging onto a tow-rope and bouncing over the waves it looked like she'd fall any second.

The threesome yelled ferociously to her.

But the skier looked over and pointed to her ear as if signaling she couldn't quite hear, or maybe she was embarrassed to be half naked and she was blowing them off. She just kept bouncing unsteadily along.

Their hopes deflated, and with the balloon deflating as well and the sharks circling, things didn't look good. To add insult to injury, the motorboat's wake swamped them.

Bull said, "She's pretty far out here to be water skiing."

Earl was surprised not to be attracted to the woman's partial nudity. He wondered if he was newly impotent.

They were sinking faster now, the weight of the cement overcoming the balloon's waning buoyancy.

"If it weren't for this darn cement," Shelby said.

"Wait!" Earl called.

"Wait for what?" Bull wiped her eyes.

"Here comes the old broad half-naked skier again!"

Sure enough, the boat and the old broad half-naked skier came by, this time much closer, almost running them over.

Shelby gave the woman the thumbs-up sign and yelled, "Tell the aircraft carrier that three Navy SEALs need to be rescued!"

The woman returned Shelby's thumbs-up sign.

"And put a shirt on!" Bull yelled.

"Admiral." Shelby looked at Bull, the boat's wake swashing her around like an eighty-five-year-old in the middle of the ocean. "That probably wasn't a wise comment to make." Then Shelby saw a massive shark fin knifing through the water's surface, headed straight for Bull. "Admiral!" She grabbed the RPG gun and whacked the shark on the snout before it had a chance to ingest Bull. Sure, Shelby thought, the shark would be disappointed (Shelby had great empathy for the hardship animals had to endure to survive in the wild) as Bull probably would've been a good meal. (Who knew how tasty, though, at that age.) But Bull was a SEAL, and the SEAL code of honor demanded Shelby save her.

And so they waited and they sank. There was no question of swimming with the cement barrels attached. Okay, Bull might've tried, but they were miles from landfall and without her glasses and sharks all over the place, it was unlikely she'd make it.

Earl was giving in to melancholic regret again. "We never should've let Manuel fill these barrels with cement."

The balloon was just about empty. Only moments till they drowned.

"Admiral." Shelby had tears in her eyes. Well, partly because the salt water was irritating them, but she was also very emotional. "I just want you to know how much I respect you, and to thank you—even though it was such a goofy plan you used—for saving us from drowning. Even though it looks like we're still going to drown."

Bull rolled her eyes. "Well, swell, Ryder."

Earl got a flash of his old self back. "Even though my balls are killing me, this is the perfect time for one last poem!"

Rather than hear another of Earl's poems, Shelby considered drowning herself, but wait, on the horizon, a Navy skiff bounced over the waves toward them. "Hey look, everybody!"

Bull spat. "I can't see diddly squat."

Earl pouted, crossed his arms and snarked, "I was about to recite a poem!"

"Later, Earl." Shelby waved her arms. That's when the machine-gun fire started, the bullets skipping off the water like fast-moving stones. "No! We're SEALs!" She held up the RPG and very quickly realized that was a bad idea.

Just then the old broad half-naked skier pulled alongside the Navy skiff. She bit down on the tow-rope handle and waved her arms, and the sailors stopped firing.

Wow, Shelby thought. That was fortunate.

But as the skiff neared, the sailors, their machine guns trained on the sinking threesome, didn't look happy. "Identify!"

"We're Navy SEALs. I'm SEAL Shelby Ryder. This…" She nodded to Earl, who was still pouting. "…is SEAL Bernstein." She looked at Bull. "And this is Rear Admiral Gompers."

The sailors looked at each other. The one smoking a pipe said through clenched teeth, "*Bull* Gompers?"

Bull took offense. "Are there any other Rear Admiral Gompers, sonny?"

The sailors didn't seem to recognize Bull. Her hair was down, and she normally wore glasses and a little hat. "But you fired an RPG at the USS *Caitlyn Jenner*, a Nimitz-class aircraft carrier, and destroyed an F-16. Clearly an act of war."

"It was an accident." Bull's tone was not happy.

Which Shelby thought was working against them. "Look, you need to help us because we're about to drown. We've got our legs in barrels filled with cement—well, with me it's just one leg, I was able to get the other leg out but that's another story—and SEAL Bernstein has suffered a severe testicular injury."

The pipe smoker narrowed his eyes at Shelby. "How did that happen?"

Shelby lowered her head and had difficulty maintaining eye contact. "Well, actually, Rear Admiral Gompers kicked him there."

The sailors looked at each other. The pipe smoker said, "*That* sounds like Bull Gompers. All right." They let down a gate, sprayed the surrounding water with machine-gun fire to keep the sharks at bay and boarded them.

Chapter Nineteen

"Look, Louie," Bull said sternly to the USS *Caitlyn Jenner*'s commanding officer. "You can dock my pay until the jet is paid off."

Bull, Shelby and Earl were sitting on the deck of the aircraft carrier being interviewed by its commanding officer, two very serious-looking MPs standing behind him at full attention. Shelby and Earl had the cement chipped off their legs, well, Shelby off only the one leg. The air was warm and the breeze brisk. Yes, the smell of jet fuel from the F16 Bull had turned into a fireball filled the air, but other than that, it was a pleasant atmosphere, and it was certainly a lot better than when they'd been surrounded by sharks and drowning.

Admiral Louis Halsey, easily Bull's age and resplendent in dress whites, a pack of gold, starry medals dangling from his breast pocket, had a steady, clear gaze in his gray eyes and sat comfortably with his white-gloved hands folded on his lap. "Bull, that jet cost eighteen million dollars. How long do you think it's going to take for you to pay that down?"

Shelby wasn't going to let Bull be browbeaten. "Admiral Halsey, sir, Bull, er, Rear Admiral Gompers, in a valiant Medal of Honor-worthy effort, risked her life to rescue SEAL Bernstein and me from a crafty little Mexican bicycle-taxi driver turned Russian spy. Sure, her rescue plan was utterly ridiculous, and yes, she kicked SEAL Bernstein in the scrotum and destroyed an F-16, but, sir, we all lived to be here to tell about it. The F-16 can be replaced, and it's not really important if SEAL Bernstein's scrotum ever recovers. In fact, if it doesn't, that would probably be a good thing."

Bull had gotten a pair of eyeglasses from the ship's

optometrist, and she looked at Shelby. "You really feel that way, Ryder?"

Shelby nodded.

Admiral Halsey nodded too. "That was a lovely story, SEAL Ryder. Very inspiring." He turned to the MPs. "Take SEAL Ryder to the brig."

An MP whisked Shelby off.

A quiet settled over the diminishing little group, the only sound being the cleanup crew hosing jet fuel off the flight deck.

Then Earl said, "If we're going to be here much longer, could I get some sunscreen?"

Admiral Halsey chuckled.

"I burn easily and have been in the sun a lot today." Earl nodded. "Any will help I suppose, but if you have SPF 50 broad spectrum that would be the best."

Admiral Halsey said, "Better yet, SEAL Bernstein, let's get you out of the sun altogether." He motioned to the other MP. "To the brig with this one too."

So the two admirals sat alone on the deck.

Bull smiled sadly. "They're good kids, Louie. Oh, they make me crazy sometimes, but yeah, they're good kids."

"I'm sure you're right, Bull." Halsey's lower lip quivered. "But you know you're all going to have to be court-martialed for this, don't you? And almost certainly you'll be de-SEALed."

"I know, Louie. I know." Bull looked down, and when she looked back up, Admiral Halsey was peering over her shoulder out to sea. "What are you looking at?"

He fingered the medals on his breast pocket. "Oh, it's just that old broad half-naked skier going by again. She's a real distraction to the men."

"Louie?"

"What, Bull?"

"Can I ask one favor?"

OOPS-A-NAVY

"Sure."

"Let us go before we're court-martialed." Bull's face lit up with entreaty. "Give us one last chance to get Senator Canfield back."

Admiral Halsey inhaled deeply and sighed. "I don't know, Bull." He looked over her shoulder again.

"The skier?"

"Yes." He gritted his teeth. "We can't stop her as she's in international waters, otherwise, I'd take her out with a Hellcat missile."

"So...the favor?"

"There's going to be an awful lot of pressure on me to see that heads roll."

"For old times' sake, Louie? For that night we spent together in that bunker in the Korean War when neither of us knew if we'd live to see the morning."

A smile emerged on Admiral Halsey's face. "I'll give you twenty-four hours."

*   *   *

"How did you swing getting the helicopter?" Shelby asked Bull as the chopper lifted off the flight deck of the USS *Caitlyn Jenner*.

Bull's face waxed nostalgic. "Louie, er, Admiral Halsey and I spent one magical night together during the Korean War."

Earl raised an eyebrow.

"Holy crap." Bull slammed her fist against the helicopter wall. "I don't know why I'm telling you two that. It must still be the hangover from that damn mushroom milkshake." She turned to Shelby. "Although, those milkshakes *were* good. Can we get those in the states?"

Shelby shrugged. "I don't know, ma'am. I'm from Kansas."

The gorgeous green-blue Caribbean Sea opened below them,

and the three of them got to talking.

Shelby said, "I can see why Admiral Halsey gave us the camouflage fatigues and body armor, but I'm surprised he gave us machine guns."

Bull crossed her arms and grunted. "What the hell, Ryder. We just made a few mistakes—we're not traitors."

"Actually, ma'am..." Shelby checked that the safety was engaged on her machine gun. "...you alone were the one who destroyed the F-16."

"All right. All right." Bull rubbed her eyes and stared out the helicopter door. "I'm the bad guy. Here comes a bad guy. Make room for the bad guy."

"Honestly, Admiral, I think we're over-weaponed for this mission." Shelby loosened the straps on her seat belt. "It's not like we're going to be in a firefight."

Bull wagged a finger in Shelby's face. "You never know, Ryder. Trust me. You never know."

Meanwhile, Earl was thinking there was a natural rhythm to some of Bull's last sentences, and that they also sounded like something from the movie *Scarface*. "You know what, Admiral, I really think you've got talent. Have you ever thought about writing poetry?"

Bull looked out the door again and sighed.

Shelby asked, squinting, "And, ma'am, why did you get a flamethrower?"

"Why, Ryder? Well, let me ask *you* this, haven't you ever seen those World War II movies where the G.I.s are pinned down by a machine-gun nest on top of a hill?"

"No."

Bull rolled her eyes. "Well, if you're pinned down like that, you need a flamethrower to take the nest out."

Earl was adapting some of Bull's recent sentences into a poem. "Hey, you two, check out this one. *I'm the bad guy / Here*

OOPS-A-NAVY

comes the bad guy / He's coming to your town / He knows how to get down."

"Bernstein, if you don't stop with the poems already..." Bull trained the flamethrower on him.

Earl's shoulders slumped. "I was just sayin'."

Shelby, sensing their sinking morale, switched the subject. "Admiral, how did you know Manuel was holding us captive? Or where we were?"

Bull laughed. "Well, when I first escaped from Doctor Cooke's medical office, I staggered around Guantanamo in a drugged daze looking for He-man."

"Hem*ana*," Shelby corrected.

"Yeah, that guy." She nodded. "But when my head finally cleared, I remembered I had a GPS receiver in my pocket that would allow me to track you and Einstein."

"Bernstein, ma'am." Earl hadn't liked her pointing the flamethrower at him and felt the need to stand up for himself.

"Hold on." Shelby made the time-out sign with perpendicular palms. "How could you possibly have tracked us with just a GPS *receiver*?"

"Ah, Ryder, that's why I'm a rear admiral and you're just a SEAL."

Earl, looking to get back at Bull for calling him Einstein again, said, "I heard the Navy brass made you admiral just because it needed to pick a woman to build up the Navy's diversity."

"Earl!" Shelby glared at him.

"Thank you, Ryder." Bull shot Earl a look too. "Anyway, how did I know where you were? Well, you two probably don't remember, but when we were in Candlebrake Cove, we did the Navy SEAL group hug."

"I remember," Earl said. "My neck still hurts from when you grabbed me there."

"Mine too," Shelby admitted.

Bull smiled wide. "That was when I planted a GPS chip into the neck of each one of you."

"Damn." Earl laughed, rubbing his neck and momentarily forgetting his resentment. "Pretty good, Admiral!"

"Thanks." The compliment seemed to rejuvenate her. She seemed less hungover from the mushroom smoothie overdose. Younger. Well, a little younger anyway. "And then once, yeah, once I sobered up enough from the mushroom milkshake, all I had to do was track you."

"But then what?" Earl's attention was rapt.

Bull nodded. "Well, I had a pound of C-4 explosive, and I was going to blow Manuel's apartment door off, but both of you certainly would've been killed. And although I didn't care if you two were killed, there would've been a nuclear war if the senator had been."

Shelby shrugged. "Okay, but what *did* you do?"

"Navy SEAL counterespionage 101, Ryder. I planted a listening device in the building's vent and overheard your plans to go to the docks to depart on *The Real Seal*. So I signed out a waterproof RPG, a heavy-duty net and a weather balloon from the Guantanamo garrison, took the frogman suit out of my duffel bag, went down to the docks, slipped into the water and waited for you three to show. Sure, soaking like that, my skin got a little pruny, but when you finally came and the boat took off, I just held onto the boat's dry-dock handle and hitched a ride."

"I gotta apologize to you, Admiral," Shelby said as the island came into view. "I told Admiral Halsey your plan was ridiculous. But really, it was ingenious."

"I know." Bull threw her shoulders back.

The helicopter veered over land now, and Bull started guiding the handsome young pilot to Manuel's. "He lives in a shantytown."

OOPS-A-NAVY

The pilot looked at her. "There are ten thousand shantytowns in Cuba."

"Okay, but this one's on a hill."

It took a lot of back and forth between them before the helicopter lowered a rope ladder to the roof of Manuel's place.

"We appreciate it, sailor!" Bull pinched the pilot's cheek and backed out of the chopper onto the rope ladder. Shelby and Earl followed suit.

The three of them stood on Manuel's roof, waving to the helicopter as it wafted away.

Bull pulled Shelby aside. "That pilot was hot, doncha think?"

Shelby figured despite what Bull had said in the chopper, she was still hung over from the mushroom smoothie, which caused its imbiber to fall in love way too easily. Either that or she was coming into puberty *very* late. "Yes, Admiral, but we really should be focusing on the mission now."

"Oh, I guess you're right, Ryder."

Earl had a giant smile on his face. He'd been busy composing yet another poem. Heedless of Bull's warning he gave it a shot. *"The helicopter dropped us off in a hurry / From us, windblown, it did scurry / We must fulfill our mission now or we'll be rued / And find the senator fast or else be screwed."*

Neither Bull nor Shelby had the energy to complain. They found a wooden ladder and climbed down from the roof.

Chapter Twenty

Bull, Shelby and Earl walked past Manuel's bicycle taxi, which was chained to a post next to his building.

Seeing Manuel's turquoise door gave Shelby flashbacks, not quite PTSD but similar. Vague images of a gorgeous Samoan man with tattoos and long curly hair, of huts and Komodo dragons, floated through her mind's eye.

Earl said, "Hey look, the door's open!"

Shelby was not pleased to have her enjoyable reverie interrupted, but indeed, the rusty lock was on the ground, the turquoise door open three or four inches.

Earl again. "I wonder if rats got in?"

Bull frowned. "I'm not worried about rats. Human rats on the other hand…" She readied the flamethrower and walked up to the door, then turned to Earl and Shelby. "This is it, SEALs. Showtime."

Earl and Shelby readied their machine guns and felt chills run up and down their spines. It was as if Bull had channeled Dirty Harry!

Bull kicked open the door, and walking in, alertly scoped the apartment. "Wow, this is some place."

"I thought so too," Shelby said. "It reminds me of the art deco stuff in South Beach."

"Yeah." Bull wielded the flamethrower around a corner and led them into the second room. "Clear!"

Earl was thinking of how the flamethrower was such a cool weapon. He'd never seen one used, though. Flamethrower Familiarity 201 was an elective class during Hell Week, and he'd always regretted not taking it.

"Look," Shelby said.

OOPS-A-NAVY

"Look at what?" Bull strained her eyes, but the glasses she'd gotten from the aircraft carrier's optometrist weren't very good. They were okay style-wise with big black frames like Oprah's, but they were maybe half the magnification of her old ones and more like the glasses people drop into those Lions Clubs collection boxes, into which a lot of color-blind people also drop their mail.

"Why, there's two half-eaten tacos and two empty beers on the table." Shelby pointed.

Earl saw an opportunity. "I wonder if there are any beers left in the fridge?"

Shelby knew they had to keep their priorities straight. They only had the twenty-four hours to get the senator back. "Mission first, Earl."

"Still." Bull finally lowered the flamethrower. "A cold one would hit the spot right now."

Shelby walked to the table. She bit into one of the tacos. "It's still warm!"

Earl pursed his lips. "Well, they're no good cold, Shelby."

"But it means whoever was here, was here not that long ago!"

"Okay!" Earl said, Shelby's enthusiasm infecting him. "Well, let's go find them!"

"Yes!" Bull agreed. "But let's check the fridge for those beers first. We're going to need to stay hydrated in this heat."

Given the justification of needing hydration, heads nodded all around.

Bull, being the highest-ranking one there, did the checking. "There's five and they're ice-cold!"

"Great!" Earl could already taste it.

Bull gave them each a beer. "All right. Are we ready to get the senator?"

Earl squinted. "Shouldn't we hydrate first?"

"You know what? That's a good suggestion, Einstein." Bull popped her brew and the others did the same.

After guzzling the beers, they were really ready to find Senator Canfield.

Bull crushed her empty can on her forehead. "Let's hit it!"

The three of them, each having passing thoughts about the two remaining beers (but how would they split them?), walked out of Manuel's. Outside, they looked up as if their eyes were drawn by a magnetic power.

A shirtless Cuban guy, a gold chain around his neck, smoking a cigar and holding a guitar stood on Manuel's roof.

Maybe, Shelby thought, he'd been the one eating tacos and drinking beer with Manuel. She raised her machine gun at him. "Identify!"

The guy slung the guitar behind his back and smiled.

Bull whispered, "These Cuban guys are so hot!"

"I'm Javier," the man said.

The SEALs introduced themselves.

"Okay, Javier." Shelby was having a hard time concentrating—the guy really was a stud and a half. "Were you eating tacos and drinking beer with Manuel recently?"

The hunk shook his head, his brown hair flowing in the breeze. "Nah. Manuel and the gringo senator were eating them. I was just playing some songs—entertaining them—but then they went to play golf."

"Hah!" Earl cried. "I knew it!"

Javier ran his hand through his hair. "They said they already had a foursome, so I couldn't go this time. Which was just as well because I have a gig in town tonight."

"Do you know what golf course they went to?" Shelby was enjoying looking into his brown eyes.

"De La Rata."

"I knew it!" Earl slapped his hip.

OOPS-A-NAVY

Shelby sighed. "Will you quit saying that, Earl?"

Bull, love in her eyes, piped up, "Where's your gig, handsome?"

"At the Diamond Cubano."

Shelby took Bull by the elbow and led her away a bit. "The mission, Admiral? Twenty-four hours? Remember?"

Only thing now was, how were they going to get to the golf course? Certainly it would be difficult, and time-consuming, walking through the shantytown in camouflage fatigues with machine guns and a flamethrower. People *could* wonder what they were up to.

Shelby scratched her head. "We can't really walk there."

"No," Bull agreed. "And after guzzling that beer, I gotta admit I'm a little groggy."

"Me too." Earl leaned against the wall. "And I might have a touch of sunstroke."

Shelby started nodding. "Are you two really saying you're quitters?"

The pep talk worked. Bull and Earl were roused to action. At least a little. But still, the problem remained—how were they going to get to De La Rata?

Javier pitched his cigar and climbed down from the roof. He seemed to intuit their dilemma. "Why don't you take Manuel's bicycle taxi? I know the combination on the lock, and I'm sure he won't mind if you borrow it."

The SEALs looked at each other. It was a no-brainer.

Javier leaned his guitar against the wall. "I can even pedal if you want."

The SEALs wanted.

While Javier removed the chain from the bicycle taxi, the SEALs examined the sidecar. With the three of them, it would be crowded, especially since they were wearing body armor and had the machine guns and flamethrower, but it was decided Bull, being the lightest, should sit on Earl's lap.

"Don't get any ideas, Einstein."

They climbed in and off they went.

The breeze generated by their descent down the hill thrilled Shelby, as did looking at Javier's back muscles rippling as he pedaled. Bull seemed excited to be so close to Javier too. She rubbed his back a few times. But Earl, well, Earl, not being attracted to Javier, was in constant pain with Bull sitting on his severely damaged scrotum, and wondering if he'd need a catheter.

As the bicycle taxi picked up speed going down the hill, they all wondered if they were going too fast.

"With all the weight in here, we're picking up a lot of speed!" Javier called.

The bicycle taxi was flying and almost to the flats when a fruit cart, loaded with bananas, pineapples, macadamia nuts, mangoes and plastic jars of jellybeans and gummy bears, rolled in front of it.

"Brace for impact!" Javier closed his eyes.

The collision sent the young Cuban stud flying from the bicycle taxi like a circus performer shot from a cannon. Bull flew as well, doing a header into the papayas. Shelby crashed into the gummy bears, and Earl into the macadamia nuts, only belatedly finding the irony in that, considering the state of *his* nuts. Needless to say, they were all, including the fruit-cart driver, disappointed.

Javier, looking hardly worse for the wear, extracted Bull from the papayas, Bull not complaining about his handling of her in the least.

Earl, sighing, said, "I say we go back for those two beers. We can split them."

Amidst the chaos, Shelby realized she had to take charge again. Pulling gummy bears from her hair—she really needed a mirror—she approached the fruit-cart driver and thrust her hand

OOPS-A-NAVY

out. "Let's see your license and registration."

The driver wore a big straw Sombrero de Yarey hat and huge sunglasses. *"Yo no hablo ingles."*

Javier came up alongside Shelby and put his arm around her shoulder. "He said he doesn't speak English."

"Oh." Shelby was so excited by the handsome Cuban's touch, her anger against the fruit-cart driver dissipated. "Well, tell him…" She put her arm around Javier's waist. "…tell him we won't press charges, but we need to commandeer his fruit cart."

Javier told the man.

"No es justo," the fruit-cart driver replied, his face flushing jalapeño red. *"Te matare si tomas mi carrito."*

Javier translated, "He said, 'That's not fair. I will kill you if you take my cart.'"

Shelby removed her arm from Javier and turned to Bull (Bull had most of the papaya wiped off). "Admiral, give me the flamethrower."

Bull did.

"Tell him," Shelby informed Javier, torching the flamethrower, a vicious column of flame jutting skyward, "not if we kill him first."

Javier told the man and he ran off.

Shelby shut down the flamethrower and surveyed the situation. The bicycle taxi was mangled beyond repair. But the fruit cart, while certainly not designed for human transportation, nonetheless held at least some promise. "We'll need several oxen to pull a rig this big." She scanned the area. "And I don't see any around."

Javier, showing some initiative, Shelby thought, talked to the little crowd of onlookers that had gathered.

"I have a better solution, Shelby," Javier, done with his conversations, said. "Several of these bystanders volunteered to pull you. They just want to know how they'll be compensated.

How much and will it be in pesos or US dollars."

Shelby looked to Bull.

Bull frowned but said, "Tell them we'll wire them each a hundred-dollar IOU backed by the full faith and credit of the United States government."

Javier told them, and the bystanders agreed to the offer.

OOPS-A-NAVY

Chapter Twenty-one

Shelby and Earl hoisted Bull into the fruit cart and then climbed in themselves. Shelby thought the cart smelled like fruit, while Earl was worried about catching the Ebola virus. With Javier and six shirtless, studly shantytown youths pulling in front, they resumed their journey to the De La Rata Country Club.

Earl, coming to think his Ebola fear was probably overblown, said, "I guess things have a way of working out after all."

"They haven't worked out yet, Einstein." Bull was trying to do something with her papaya-caked hair. "If we don't get the senator back, we'll be court-martialed, and we might even end up in Leavenworth."

Earl squirmed. "Leavenworth Prison?"

"Uh-huh."

Shelby shrugged. "At least it's in Kansas."

Earl frowned. "That makes it worse."

Shelby blew the bangs off her forehead. "I don't know. This whole thing is beginning to seem crazy. We started at Guantanamo, thinking the senator was there. Then we heard he's in Candlebrake Cove, and so we go there—and get drugged with hallucinogenic mushroom smoothies and think we see multiple versions of him. (And multiple Elvises.) Then it turns out Manuel, the smallish but morally upright Cuban bicycle-taxi driver, is actually a Mexican-turned-Russian spy. And now there's the half-eaten tacos, and Javier says Manuel and the senator just went to play golf. None of those things are connected and none of them make any sense."

Bull switched off the dual safeties on the flamethrower. "Welcome to the life of a Navy SEAL, Ryder. Where you never know what sort of strange mission you'll be called on to complete, and *nothing* ever goes down easy. Now, if you two are smart..." She turned to Shelby and Earl. "...you best prepare for one hell of a confrontation."

They rolled alongside the jungle, Javier and the shantytown youths' backs bent, sweat pouring down their golden torsos. Shelby and Earl were thinking nostalgically about the happy times they'd spent at their base camp tent there. Of course, there'd been the boa constrictor, the croc and the altercation with the cannibals, but they tended to block that out.

"Earl, are you glad you became a SEAL instead of a proctologist?" The anticipation of the mortal danger awaiting them softened her toward him. She smiled.

Earl stretched leisurely. "You know, Shelby, I really am. Being a proctologist would've been more lucrative, and my parents would've been happy to have me living at home with them, but look at all the excitement I would've missed out on."

"Huh."

"How about you, Shelby? Are you glad you're a SEAL?"

"Well." She leaned on his shoulder. "Being from Kansas it's a big relief to be anything other than from Kansas, but what drives me is my desire to avenge my parents, and the SEALs give me my best chance of getting it."

Earl put his arm around her. "You know, if I wasn't so hot for you all the time, I'd almost think of you as a sister."

"Aww, Earl." Shelby, knowing Earl's testicles were prohibitively impaired, even snuggled against him. "That's almost a nice thing to say."

Bull commanded, "You two numbnuts—quit your jabbering and lock and load those machine guns."

They were at the golf course. The huge rolling green property alongside the ocean was like a Shangri-La materializing out of the jungle. The palm trees along the golden sand bent in the breeze blowing in off the ocean. The breakers rolled in endlessly. And

OOPS-A-NAVY

golfers were everywhere, riding their carts, hitting golf shots, making putts and having fun, oblivious to the suffering of the rest of the world. Yes, golfers were everywhere. Only where were Manuel and Senator Canfield? The SEALs strained their eyes. (Bull with the inferior new glasses wasn't much help in that regard.) This was it. They had to find them. Everything was on the line.

Shelby told Javier and the rest of the cart pullers that this was good where they were, especially since a sign read FRUIT CARTS POSITIVELY NOT ALLOWED ON GOLF COURSE. The SEALs would have to advance on foot. Shelby thanked Javier and the sweaty shantytown youths for their service, gave them her address so they could write to collect the IOUs and told them to visit if they were ever in Kansas.

She jumped out of the fruit cart and made sure the safety was off on her machine gun. "The time has come, SEALs."

Bull seemed woebegone watching the sweaty Cuban studs swagger away, but the old broad knew how to suck it up. "SEALs forever!"

Earl was finally playing ball. "Yeah! SEALs forever!"

Guerrilla-like they marched onto the fifth hole, which was named Little Iguana (no one really knew why). The heavily armed SEALs were drawing stares from the golfers, but so far so good—they hadn't had to kill any of them. But still, no Senator Canfield and Manuel. They walked through a little tunnel, alarming a couple of black golfers on the other end and emerged on the sixth hole, which was known as Medium Iguana, the hole's name most probably derived from the hole being bigger than Little Iguana but not by much. The hole was in a valley and surrounded by a ridge, giving it the appearance of being in a bowl.

Shelby, on point and checking for IEDs, saw them first. She almost fainted. From the middle of the fairway, two golf carts raced toward them. In one sat the Harringtons, and in the other, Senator Canfield and someone who looked to be Manuel. But he had no mustache! Yet it was Manuel. Or was it? "Earl, is that Manuel?"

"Not sure, Shelby," Earl said squinting. "I don't see his mustache."

"Exactly."

Bull torched the flamethrower and yelled, "Stop your vehicles right now or we will kill you!"

But the carts kept coming. Bull leveled the flamethrower, Shelby and Earl leveling their machine guns as well.

The carts finally stopped. Bull killed the flamethrower. Shelby thought Senator Canfield looked nice—but he always looked nice—in a lime-green Polo shirt. Preston looked the CEO in a crisp gray shirt. And Ashley was her usual buff self in a maroon sleeveless top. While Manuel, or the guy who looked like him, was the fashion dud of the group in an army-green uniform and cap. But really, Shelby reprimanded herself, this was no time to be assessing their fashion style.

Ashley called out, "Shelby, Earl and Bull, nice to see you, but what's with the heavy weaponry and why are you threatening to kill us?"

"It's clearly unacceptable," Preston added.

Shelby wasn't intimidated. After all, she, Earl and Bull had the heavy weaponry. "Why don't you ask Manuel?"

"Where's Manuel?" The affable Senator Canfield looked around.

"He's sitting right next to you, Senator," Earl yelled.

Senator Canfield turned and looked deeply at the man next to him before turning back to the SEALs. "Are you referring to First Secretary Perez?" He affectionately squeezed the man's shoulder.

"Don't be fooled, Senator. He's not First Secretary Anything. He's a little Mexican-turned-Russian spy named Manuel. He's the

OOPS-A-NAVY

same guy who held you hostage." Shelby waved her machine gun. "Now get out of the cart right now and with your hands up walk slowly toward us. As you know, sir, we're Navy SEALs and sworn to uphold the Constitution of the United States. You'll be safe with us."

"Why, that's utter nonsense." The senator crossed his arms over his chest and clenched his jaw. "I'm perfectly safe in the first secretary's company."

"Okay, Manuel," Shelby yelled. "So you shaved your mustache, but go ahead and tell them who you are!"

The man calmly puffed on a cigar and said, "I am First Secretary Raul Perez of Cuba."

"Ha ha ha," Earl called, remembering being abducted by Manuel and then later getting kicked in the balls. (They still hurt.) True, the kick was from Bull, but it never would've happened had Manuel not abducted them. "Nice try, you little homunculus."

"You really think I am not First Secretary Perez?" The self-righteous anger in the man's voice was unmistakable.

Shelby thought Earl's homunculus slur, although certainly accurate, was counterproductive. In hotbed negotiations, people needed to be made to feel good about themselves.

The man with the questionable identity grabbed a cell phone.

"Put the phone down now!" Shelby knew he might be detonating an IED right where the SEALs stood.

Leisurely, so very leisurely, the man finished his conversation and then flipped his phone shut. He puffed on his cigar. "Now you will see who I am."

Like night emerging, from one side of the ridge surrounding Medium Iguana thousands of Cuban soldiers appeared. Like Indians overwhelming the Cavalry. They were massively armed. And Shelby could see several of them setting up a machine-gun nest.

Manuel, or the Manuel-like man, shouted, "Everybody

down!"

The Harringtons, Senator Canfield and Manuel or the Manuel-like man dropped to the verdant green earth and rolled under their golf carts.

The Cubans on the ridge started shooting.

"Quick!" Shelby knew they didn't have a lot of time. She grabbed Bull and Earl and they ran. "C'mon, into that sand trap!"

Several bullets hit the SEALs' body armor, but the threesome made it to the cavernous sand trap. With the appearance of the massively armed Cuban horde, though, they were to a man—well to a man and two women—thinking that maybe that hadn't been Manuel in the golf cart after all. But they were also thinking this wasn't the time to ponder that as machine-gun bullets zipped over their heads. Earl and Shelby returned fire, picking off several hundred of the Cubans, but they were pinned down, and with at least ten thousand Cubans on the ridge, they would run out of ammo before they could kill them all. And the machine-gun nest's withering assault from the top of the ridge would soon obliterate the cover the sand trap afforded them.

Bull crawled between Earl and Shelby. "You two cover me, and I think I can get to that machine-gun nest and take it out."

"Hmm." Shelby thought that would be really interesting to see. But the angels of her better nature took over. "Sounds too risky."

Earl, tired of Bull calling him Einstein, considered telling her to go for it, but hey, she was a SEAL after all. "Admiral, that's a suicide mission. You'll never make it."

"All right, you whippersnappers." Bull made sure she had their eyes. "Now do you think Bull is my real name?"

Earl nodded. Shelby too.

"No! It's Bertha! Bull's a nickname. Know how I got it?"

Earl shook his head. Shelby too.

"Storming a machine-gun nest with a flamethrower! Now

OOPS-A-NAVY

cover me!" Bull climbed over the top of the sand trap and started running.

Earl and Shelby stood, blasting the merciless Cubans, but also making sure to aim over Bull's head. Killing Bull with friendly fire, while gratifying in many ways, would almost certainly get them de-SEALed.

Bull made it to the golf cart with the Harringtons under it. "Now just stay calm, Ashley and Preston. We'll have this under control real soon."

"Bull." Preston looked at her. "Listen to me. That really is First Secretary Raul Perez under the other golf cart."

"Well, okay, Preston, I'll take your word for it, and I won't torch the guy. But these others." She glanced up at the machine-gun nest. "These others have acted as aggressors against the United States Navy, and under the Geneva Convention's Rules of War we are authorized—in fact, we are obligated—to engage them with deadly force."

Preston said, "Okay, Bull, if those are the rules, those are the rules."

"They are, Preston." Bull waved to Earl and Shelby that she was ready to advance. So Earl and Shelby let loose with a barrage of machine-gun fire, and Bull broke for the ridge, atop of which sat the machine-gun nest. But the ridge was steeper than she thought and it took her longer to get up it.

Back at the sand trap, Earl and Shelby had to stop shooting because they were afraid with Bull being so far up the ridge they'd hit her.

Bull, exhausted, sweaty, and not seeing so clearly because she had the inferior glasses, sparked the flamethrower and, flames shooting out from it like a dragon's breath, ran up the hill yelling, "AAAAAAAaaaaahhhhhhhh! Navy SEALs forever!"

The nest torched—and unhappy Cubans afire running helter-skelter—its deadly machine gun silenced, Bull dropped the flamethrower and rolled down the ridge all the way back to the sand trap.

"Great job, Admiral!" Shelby said, and along with Earl, hugged her. "When the machine-gun nest was torched, the Cubans retreated. We've won!"

Done hugging, they stood and surveyed the situation. The Harringtons, the senator and the man who might be Manuel crawled from under their golf carts and drove off.

Earl readied his weapon. "I can shoot out their tires."

"No." Bull lowered the barrel of Earl's machine gun. "I learned some disturbing news."

Chapter Twenty-two

Things fell into, or depending on one's perspective, out of place quickly after that. Senator Canfield returned to the US to a hero's welcome. The dominant theme in the media was that he was the beneficiary of the president's brilliant diplomatic intervention. There was no mention of the Navy SEALs' efforts involved in securing his release. In fact, whatever press related to the SEALs' involvement condemned them for acting outside of their jurisdiction and illegally breaching Cuba's sovereignty. They were called "bad apples" and "rogue agents." It was clear to Bull, Shelby and Earl that they'd been set up. Patsies.

And so it was a long boat ride back to the mainland in the crappy fishing trawler Fleet Admiral Kazinski sent for them. How you traveled in the Navy was a clue to the regard the big brass had for you. The highly favored shuttled around in lightning fast, luxurious Navy jets. The disregarded in-the-doghouse SEALs, in sluggish boats barely seaworthy.

"You know what, *I* actually think we did great." Shelby leaned up against the wall in their cabin as the boat endlessly rode up and down the waves on its way across the Florida Straits. "We treated the indigenous kindly. We exposed a cult in Candlebrake Cove. *And* we found Senator Canfield and averted a nuclear war. The Navy brass wanting to court-martial us really missed the call on this one."

Earl was eating a tamale. "How were we to know that guy really was the first secretary of Cuba? He looked just like Manuel."

Bull was resting in a hammock, which swayed with the rise and fall of the trawler. "I never knew what Manuel looked like and so had no way of knowing, but I wouldn't have been able to identify him one way or another with those crappy glasses they gave me."

"I still can't get over it." Shelby sighed. "And after Javier—"

"He was a hottie," Bull interrupted.

"—told us Manuel went to play golf with the senator. I mean, after all that, what were the odds that the guy wasn't Manuel?"

"Astronomical." Earl felt like he had tamale stuck between his molars on the lower right side. "*And* the little homunculus got away."

Sighing, Shelby said, "With the locket my parents gave me."

"The media are calling us mercenaries, assassins." Earl picked at the stuck tamale but didn't want to cause any gum bleeding. "And 736 Cubans dead in that firefight. I saw in one newspaper they were calling it the Massacre of Medium Iguana Ridge."

"That was unfortunate PR, for sure," Bull said. "But they *were* trying to kill us."

"So now it's home to face de-SEALment and probably Leavenworth Prison." Shelby frowned. "It's outrageous."

"Pffft." Bull sat up in the hammock. "You know that. I know that. Bernstein knows that. But they don't care in Washington. The president had his story of what happened and stuck with it. But I have a feeling I know what really happened."

Earl finished the tamale. He could hardly wait to floss out the part that got stuck—*if* it came out—but he was curious to hear what Bull had to say. "What, Admiral?"

"Can I trust you two?" Even though she couldn't see that well with the crappy glasses, she eyed Earl and Shelby as best she could. "If this gets out, I could be accused of treason and executed."

Shelby shrugged. Hmm. She's eighty-five. That would hardly be so tragic. It reminded her of an article she'd read in a magazine about a woman who was a hundred and five that quit smoking

OOPS-A-NAVY

because she was afraid it would shorten her life. "Admiral, I wouldn't worry about that at your stage of living."

"I disagree, Ryder." Bull pressed her lips together and rolled out of the hammock, falling onto the floor, but she quickly jumped up into a chair as if she'd meant to do things that way. "You know what they're saying—eighty-five is the new fifty-five."

Earl was searching in his backpack for dental floss. "I never heard that."

"Well, I did, Einstein."

"Come on you two." Shelby took charge. "All right, Admiral, we're sworn to secrecy. What's your explanation?"

"It's simple. The president *bought* his re-election by paying off Senator Canfield."

Shelby smirked. "How did he *buy it*?"

"Okay." Bull clasped her hands together. "The president knew Senator Canfield would beat him if he ran, so he gave him an offer he couldn't refuse. He paid him off—probably millions—and shunted him off to Cuba on a golfing trip. But the senator couldn't just play golf until after the election, so to make things more plausible, the president's fixers eventually came up with their cockamamie story of him being abducted by the commies. They had us there to show that they were doing *something* to find him, but they never wanted us to find him until *after* the election. Senator Canfield was probably just in the nearby Dominican Republic where they have much nicer golf courses, and he returned to Cuba right after the election. But then he really did end up getting abducted."

"Wow." Earl wedged the floss between the suspect teeth but wasn't a hundred percent sure he'd gotten all the tamale out.

"Well, that make sense." Shelby clenched her fists. "And it explains why we couldn't find him at first."

Bull nodded. "Exactly."

The veins throbbed in Shelby's forehead. "I tell you what, though. Life's not fair. Here we saved the day—we're heroes really—and now we're heading home to de-SEALment and prison."

"Well, we don't know that for certain, Ryder." Bull took off her crappy glasses and sighed. "But it sure looks that way."

The End

ABOUT THE AUTHOR

Gregg Bell writes mostly thrillers. Some funny. Some serious.

Born in Chicago, he's sold puka shells on the beach in Florida, worked for Sears in their corporate headquarters at Sears Tower, and done just about everything in between. He lives in suburban Chicago.

Website: greggbell.net

Also by Gregg Bell

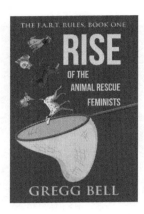

Lainey Tripper is a whiskey-drinking hard-living animal rescue feminist. But she has just this one little problem: she can't seem to stop killing men. Not all men are so bad, and not a few of them are attracted to her, but when Lainey leaves a rescue, dead men are invariably left in her wake.

Lainey heads FART (Feminist Animal Rescue Team), a group of women dedicated to stopping the villainous Donovan from oppressing women and animals. But now Donovan, intent on world domination, has taken his evil to a new level. He's systematically stealing Chicago's dogs to sell them to a foreign power. In Lainey's enthusiasm to stop Donovan, she again kills a lot of men. Her fellow FARTers plead with her to moderate her man-killing tendencies, but Lainey's pretty sure any guy she kills deserves it, and besides, she must do whatever it takes to save Chicago's dogs.

Will Lainey stop Donovan in time? And when she's done, will any men be left alive?

OOPS-A-NAVY

See all Gregg's novels and more at his web site:

greggbell.net

GREGG BELL

Oops-A-Navy

Copyright © 2018 by Gregg Bell

Published by: Thriveco, Inc.
207 North Walnut Street, Itasca, IL 60143
All Rights Reserved

ISBN-13: 978-1721277216

Without limiting the rights under the copyright reserved above, no part of this publication may be reproduced, stored in or introduced into a retrieval system, or transmitted, in any form, or by any means (electronic, mechanical, photocopying, recording, or otherwise), without the prior written permission of both the copyright owner and the above publisher of this book.

This is a work of fiction. Names, characters, places, and incidents either are the products of the author's imagination or are used fictitiously, and any resemblance to actual persons, living or dead, events, or locales is entirely coincidental.

The author is not, nor has ever been a Navy SEAL nor a member of any armed forces.

17618

Made in the USA
Middletown, DE
12 August 2018